Television Newsfilm Techniques

TELEVISION NEWSFILM TECHNIQUES

by

Vernon Stone and Bruce Hinson

A Project of
The Radio Television News Directors Association

COMMUNICATION ARTS BOOKS

Hastings House, Publishers • New York 10016

To Saribenne and Doris

Copyright © 1974
by the Radio Television News Directors Association

First published, August 1974
Reprinted, October 1978
Library of Congress Cataloging in Publication Data
Stone, Vernon.
   Television newsfilm techniques.
   (Communication arts books)
   "A project of the Radio Television News Directors Association."
   1. Newsreel.   2. Television broadcasting of news.
I. Hinson, Bruce, joint author.   II. Radio Television News
Directors Association.   III. Title.
TR895.S76   1974   070.1'9   74-6336
ISBN 0-8038-7139-2
ISBN 0-8038-7141-4 (pbk.)

Published simultaneously in Canada
by Saunders of Toronto, Ltd., Don Mills, Ontario

Designed by Al Lichtenberg
Drawings by Deborah Hayes
WOTV photos by Jo Keener
Printed in the United States of America

Contents

    Sound-on-Film Equipment
    Voice Sound
    Natural Sound
    Wild Sound

6   CAMERA REPORTING   82
    Equipment in the Field
    Getting the Story
    Types of Stories
    Documentaries

7   EDITING NEWSFILM   107
    Why Edit?
    Equipment
    Procedure
    Film Language
    Basic Sound-on-Film
    Sound with B-Roll
    Double-System Sound
    With Audio Tape
    Editorial Decisions

8   WRITING FOR NEWSFILM   134
    Coordination with Editing
    Writing for Silent Film
    Writing for Sound Film
    Writing Style

9   FILM PROCESSING   148

10 NEW TOOLS FOR CAMERA REPORTING   155
    Portable Electronic Cameras
    Super 8

11 TRENDS: FROM NEWSREEL TO NEWS REALITY   163

    Appendix: RTNDA Code of Broadcast News Ethics   173

    Glossary   177

    Index   187

Preface

This book was written in response to needs expressed by members of the Radio Television News Directors Association and others for (1) a primer to reduce the "instructional" time required in the training of newcomers, and (2) a source of information on newsfilm practices and trends to serve anyone who works in or is a student of television news. The overall objective of this publication, as of others generated by RTNDA, is the improvement of standards and performance in the profession of broadcast journalism.

Such improvement is a major purpose of RTNDA, a professional organization of more than 1,000 broadcast journalists. Although primarily for news directors, who are the persons in charge of radio and television news operations, RTNDA membership includes many other news men and women, broadcast journalism educators and professionals in other broadcast news-related fields. There are members from television and radio networks and news services as well as from stations. Membership is international, mainly in the United States and Canada but including broadcast journalists in several other countries. Members pledge themselves to a code of journalistic ethics (included in this book's appendix) and generally work for leading broadcast news operations in all sizes of stations and markets.

Originally, RTNDA planned to publish only a manual on shooting silent film. But the subject matter was expanded to meet other needs expressed in a survey conducted by Vernon Stone in summer of 1973.

9

To ascertain needed content for the book, questionnaires were mailed to the 231 television station news directors then listed as members of RTNDA, for completion by "the person in charge of newsfilm." Respondents totalled 165, for a response rate of 71%. The survey was not designed to represent all stations (about 630 commercial TV stations were originating news programs in 1973), but only the 37% with news directors who were members of RTNDA at the time. This limits the generalizability of the survey data, but is consistent with the objective of gathering information from stations where high newsfilm standards matter.

As the majority of survey respondents said should be done, all aspects of newsfilm are covered in this book. Especially in small and medium markets, most members of typical news staffs may be called upon to do every job involved in the newsfilm operation.

Many newsfilm techniques can be self-taught to a great extent. An instructor need not be present during most of the learning process. News directors, chief photographers and professors have better things to do than needless spoon-feeding. Besides, many beginners prefer being left alone to figure things out for themselves, with the help of a written guide. With a copy of this book, we hope, newcomers can learn much of what they need to know on their own.

We start with the assumptions that the student or beginning staffer has never before touched a movie camera, but wants to learn newsfilm and is willing to invest the necessary time, study, concentration, alertness and practice—lots of it. With this book as a training guide, with feedback from a seasoned professional, and with a serious, self-critical attitude, the beginner—or the experienced practitioner whose work needs improvement—should be on the way to using television newsfilm as the powerful reportorial medium which it can be.

Techniques are presented in the instructional order which has worked best for the authors and colleagues over many years of helping newsroom and classroom beginners develop into TV newsfilm journalists. The first step should be learning the basic equipment of camera reporting. Next comes the use of these newsfilm tools to cover stories in field situations. Then we move to the editing table to finish turning the film into stories. Finally, we look to a future which promises greater use of portable electronic cameras and perhaps super 8 film in television news.

The book is intended for classrooms as well as newsrooms. Television newsfilm is a central area of instruction in an up-to-date program of broadcast journalism education.

A station-level rather than network-level approach is taken. While much of the best newsfilm work is done by the networks, information on techniques is most needed at the station level. It is here, too, that students using the book will get their first jobs.

Our topic is newsfilm reporting, not "filmmaking" in the broader sense. Whether for a 45-second clip or an hour-long documentary, film is treated here as a reportorial tool. Newsfilm should primarily reflect the reality of the event or situation, not a reporter's preconceptions or a filmmaker's artistic inclinations.

All techniques are as applicable to documentaries as to shorter newsfilm stories.

Techniques are presented from the standpoint of the film journalist rather than the technical specialist. Terms, definitions and recommendations are those which are common in the television news profession and in some cases may not satisfy the cinematographic purist. Most readers will not make careers of newsfilm but will work with it only as one of many aspects of television news. Thus, most of the book deals with technical matters only at an elementary level and is not intended as more than a primer for those who plan to specialize in film. Other books and manuals are available for detailed technical treatment of such topics as film characteristics, optics and camera mechanisms.

News directors and others experienced in newsfilm should find the book useful as a refresher, a collection of varied points of view from other news operations, and a future-oriented report on newsfilm trends. Top professionals who participated in the RTNDA survey are quoted throughout the book.

This RTNDA project had many contributors. A substantial portion of the content consists of comments and examples from RTNDA news directors and members of their staffs. Many who helped must go unacknowledged. In addition to those cited in the text, we wish particularly to thank: Benedict Kruse, Frank Associates; Bos Johnson, WSAZ-TV, Huntington, W. Va.; James Hoyt, Thomas Beell and Mary Ann Coffman, University of Wisconsin; Larry Walklin, Peter Mayeux and Ed Bailey, University of Nebraska; Ernie Schultz, WKY-TV, Oklahoma City; Pete Fenney, WHA-TV, Madison, Wis.; Jon McCall, WMTV, Madison; Norb Tatro, WTMJ-TV, Milwaukee; Bob Homberg, WITI-TV, Milwaukee; and Travis Linn, who was at WFAA-TV, Dallas, when his efforts revived the project and moved it toward completion.

The authors take full responsibility for the content of the book. Although a project of RTNDA, its *content does not necessarily represent the views of the organization.* The only part approved as official RTNDA policy is the Code of Broadcast News Ethics in the appendix.

References to brands or models of equipment do not in any way constitute endorsement by RTNDA or the authors and are not to be so represented in any advertising or promotion.

Especially since the book has so many contributors, we do not expect all professionals to agree with everything written herein, any more than they agree among themselves on all techniques.

Furthermore, this book—like any other—should be used only as a takeoff point. It is hoped that you will find better ways of doing things than some we describe. The authors have changed attitudes and approaches regarding various newsfilm techniques over the years. Otherwise, we would be terribly out of date. Television is a changing profession which should always be open to more effective ways of communicating the realities of a changing world.

April 1974

Vernon Stone
Bruce Hinson

1 | Why Learn Newsfilm?

Why should you learn television newsfilm techniques? The answer is simple. A knowledge of newsfilm basics is either necessary or helpful for most jobs in television news. Film is the primary element in the reporting of the sights and sounds of news for which television is uniquely qualified. Whatever you do—whether actually shooting or editing film, or writing, reporting or producing for TV news—your job will be related to the use of cameras to bring the viewer the pictures and sounds of reality.

How can you use the training? Unless working for a network or highly unionized major-market station, you will very likely be expected to shoot or edit newsfilm either regularly or occasionally. High specialization is the exception rather than the rule in TV news. Most members of typical news staffs do a little of everything. A 1972 survey of television news operations headed by members of the Radio Television News Directors Association showed that most people were doing multiple jobs at more than half of the stations. One-third reported moderately specialized staffs, and only 8% said that most members of their staffs were highly specialized.

Even the large, unionized operations in which work is highly specialized prefer to hire TV journalists who have "done everything" in previous jobs at smaller stations. Although the network correspondents seen on TV do not normally shoot or edit newsfilm, many of them have done so in earlier years. As examples, David Dick and

SIGNIFICANT NEWS STORIES on community problems can be as challenging as fire coverage. Carroll Darringer films an interview by Vance Coleman for WMT-TV, Cedar Rapids, Iowa. Though serving as reporter on this particular story, Coleman can also shoot, edit and write for newsfilm. This is the case for most members of typical TV news staffs.

WHEN NEWS BREAKS, newsfilm photographers like James Priest, KTRK, Houston, are soon on the scene, sometimes suddenly called into action on a day off. Filming a fire may be hazardous as well as exciting.

Richard Threlkeld are among the CBS correspondents with newsfilm backgrounds, Dick at WHAS-TV, Louisville, and Threlkeld at WMT-TV, Cedar Rapids. Reporters and correspondents tend to work better with newsfilm photographers and editors when they have gained experience in those roles themselves.

Television news directors can gain from first-hand knowledge of newsfilm techniques. Many came to their present jobs with newsfilm backgrounds—for example, Jim Reiman, KRON-TV, San Francisco, and Wayne Vriesman, KWGN-TV, Denver, who are among the RTNDA contributors to this book. Others—like Bill Small, senior vice president and director of news for CBS News—learned newsfilm basics after becoming news executives. One of the first things Small did upon assuming an earlier position as news director at WHAS-TV was to learn to shoot newsfilm. Small did this, not because he planned a newsfilm career, but because he wanted a basic orientation in everything he asked his staff to do.

Is it satisfying work? Yes, for those who develop the ability and a real feeling for it. Once you experience how effectively reporting can be done with TV newsfilm, you may become like Ed Dooks of WBZ-TV, Boston, (quoted extensively in Chapter 6) who probably would not exchange newsfilm work for a desk job under any circumstances. Many film journalists simply would not be happy doing anything else. And quite a few who have become news executives or professors find themselves working with film when it's not really necessary—just because they can't stay away from it.

There is an inherent excitement about a political contest, an interview with a controversial newsmaker, a fire or flood, a basketball game, or even Christmas shopping. The excitement becomes more real when you are putting the event on film as the first step in communicating this segment of reality to the public.

Editing film can also be satisfying. Much of the effectiveness of a newsfilm story or documentary may result from the selection, trimming and rearranging of film scenes at the editing table. Even when bad film among the good makes the unedited version look hopeless, a skillful editor may come up with a high quality final product. Meeting such editing challenges is enjoyable for the person with a feeling for the many ways pictures and sounds can be used to tell news stories and document reality on television.

But isn't it demanding? It certainly is. And don't get into newsfilm—or any other job in television news—unless you can carry out assignments under adverse conditions. The work often carries more strain than glamour. It is not uncommon for camera reporters to be confronted with hostility, threats, and even violence. There are parts of reality which are relevant to the public but which participants would prefer not to have shown. In addition, when things go wrong, some people find it easy to blame television. As Bill Small put it in his book *To Kill a Messenger: Television News and the Real World* (Hastings House, 1970), "The public has turned its anger on the messenger, the bearer of bad tidings." (page xi).

You must be quick-thinking and able to work under pressure. If turned away from a police checkpoint, do you give up? Or do you quickly think of tactics which might get you in? If demonstrators or police charge after you and your camera, what do you do? In some situations, it's either a cool head or a battered one. And what if late newsfilm comes out of the processor only 10 minutes before airtime and needs 30 minutes of editing? If you are suited for the TV news profession, you will figure a way to get the film edited into air-worthy form in 10 minutes.

What of career opportunities? Stations are always looking for camera reporters who can tell stories effectively with film. For a highly unionized station, this may mean strictly newsfilm photography. But for a typical station, you may often serve as reporter as well as photographer, especially on silent film stories. Professional advancement will depend upon such factors as your skill, drive, enterprise, dependability and ability to work with others.

Should you decide to make a career of newsfilm or documentary, you may become a chief photographer or documentary film producer. News documentaries are essentially an extension of the basic newsfilm reporting treated in this book.

You may become a television reporter, working more often in front of than behind the camera.

Or having proved yourself with newsfilm in the field, you may move to a newsroom job such as assignment editor, assistant news director, or even news director.

Newsfilm experience may also bring opportunities in news-related professions, such as public relations for a company or governmental agency. PR is becoming increasingly aware of television's impact and is creating more jobs for persons trained and experienced in newsfilm.

Whether to make a career of newsfilm is a decision you may well defer. The best advice for most beginners is to seek a news job with a small or medium sized station where you will get to do a little of everything—newsfilm shooting and editing, writing, reporting and, ideally, some on-the-air work. With such experience, you will be better qualified to decide in which, if any, area of television news to become a specialist.

Are members of minorities welcome? Yes. As this was being written, many TV stations were not only welcoming—but were seeking out—

NEWSFILM EDITING can be a satisfying assignment. Editors like Joanne Williams, WTMJ-TV, Milwaukee, select, trim and rearrange scenes to help film tell stories in the most effective way.

ASSIGNMENT EDITORS and others who make decisions on newsfilm need first-hand experience in it. Tom Rippe, WITI-TV, Milwaukee, coordinates newsfilm reporting in the field by telephone and by two-way radio contact with station vehicles.

black persons and members of other minorities for jobs in newsfilm and other areas of broadcast journalism. Stations were taking affirmative action to correct a situation in which television news, like many other professions, had for many years consisted almost exclusively of white males.

Black persons, Spanish Americans, American Indians or Asian Americans were working in nearly two-thirds of the nation's TV news operations in 1972, according to a survey by Stone.

Forty per cent of these minority members of news staffs were working with newsfilm, according to a follow-up survey conducted in 1973 by Stone and graduate student Tracy Regan.

Most (82%) of the news directors and two-thirds of the minority employees said they felt that being members of minorities helped those employees get the jobs. Practically no one said it hindered.

Several news directors indicated that they had originally hired minority personnel because of governmental or other pressures, but later found that race or national origin is in fact irrelevant to a person's ability to do a job. As such enlightened attitudes become more prevalent, television news is moving increasingly toward truly equal opportunities.

What if you are a woman? That, too, is irrelevant at a growing number of the better stations. At these stations, news personnel are hired, assigned and promoted on the basis of individual ability rather than whether they were born male or female. If you are a woman interested in newsfilm, documentary or any other job in television, you deserve and should demand equal opportunity with men of comparable ability. As is the case with minorities, you have the legal backing of the U.S. Constitution and the Federal Communications Commission.

And you have the professional support of an increasing number of news directors. About half of the nation's RTNDA news directors surveyed by Stone in 1972 said they believed a woman "of comparable ability" could shoot newsfilm as well as a man. Four of every five said a woman could edit film as well as a man, and practically all said a woman could do as well as a man in writing or reporting.

Many of those expressing reservations about sending a woman out to shoot newsfilm said this was only because sound-on-film equipment was so heavy. With the lightweight cameras now available, that should no longer be a problem—if it ever was. The old description of women as the "weaker sex" is largely nonsense anyway.

As this was being written *news*women (excluding secretaries and clerical workers) were employed in more than half of the TV news operations in the United States, several women had become news directors, and the membership of RTNDA included a substantial number of women for the first time.

Female or male, beginner or executive, if you are truly interested in television news, there are plenty of good reasons to learn all you can about newsfilm techniques. Television news encompasses the sights and sounds of events. Newsfilm and tape, to a large extent, are the vehicles by which we communicate this reality.

SUMMARY

- Everyone working in television news needs a basic knowledge of newsfilm techniques.
- The work can be satisfying but is demanding. Any television journalist must keep a cool head and get jobs done under pressure.
- Career opportunities are good. Newsfilm experience is excellent background for top positions in TV news.
- Being a woman or a member of a minority group is irrelevant to one's employment and assignments at an increasing number of stations.

2 | Camera Operation

Don't be overwhelmed. Newsfilm equipment is easy to use, once you understand it.

But don't be over-confident. Failure to fully learn the camera and how to use it will result in amateurish, probably unusable film. The learning will take time and lots of practice.

Learn everything thoroughly, then go over it all again. Over-learning at this stage is the secret to the proficiency which can later free you from having to worry about camera mechanics when you should be concentrating on the job of camera reporting. Learn to handle the camera, load and unload it, set lenses correctly, and take basic shots so well now that these things will be approaching second nature by the time you shoot your first film. You should then come back with film good enough for use on the air—your first time out—instead of sad stories about "human error" or just being a "beginner."

Get to know the camera before loading it with fresh film. You can master the mechanics of the camera and related equipment before doing any actual shooting. After several hours of practicing with the equipment, you should be able to shoot usable film your first time out. If not, spend some more time with the empty camera.

Reading this and subsequent chapters will be enhanced by having a 16mm motion picture camera nearby for reference. Ideally it should be equipped with a full complement of three lenses (wide angle, 1-inch and telephoto) or a zoom lens. A manufacturer's manual for the camera will be helpful. Access to other equipment related to later chapters is also recommended.

USING SILENT CAMERAS

Although a number of stations are moving almost totally to sound film, the initial learning is best accomplished with a silent camera. Most of the techniques used for silent newsfilm will also apply to your later shooting with sound. For that matter, silent film will continue to be shot by most stations for some time to come. Indeed, for some film— for example, aerials in which the sound of the aircraft is not part of the story—silent film may be preferred.

The basic frame of reference in this chapter is the Bell & Howell 70DR, the most-used silent camera at most stations when this book was written. But a Canon Scoopic, Bolex or other camera will serve your needs as well. Most of the important principles apply to all cameras.

Handling a Camera

Handle a camera like the precision instrument it is. Though fairly rugged, it can easily have to go back to the factory for costly repairs because of inept or careless handling. Don't place a camera where it can fall or be dropped. When placing it on a table or shelf, put it flat side down and back from the edge. Check occasionally to be sure the strap is in good condition. If carrying the camera swinging at your side, let the back face forward as a precaution against bumping into something with the delicate lenses.

The steadiest, most secure way for most people to hold a camera is the one recommended by the manufacturer. For the Bell & Howell, this means gripping the fingers of the left hand over the viewfinder barrel, with the adjustable strap over the back of the hand (thumb out) while the base of the hand braces the camera. Most people use the second or third fingers of the right hand for triggering the camera with the button on top. The rest of the hand becomes a brace. Bell & Howell recommends that you brace the camera against the forehead and look through the viewfinder with the left eye. This maximizes stability for B&H 70 cameras and concentrates attention through the viewfinder by partially blocking extraneous view from the right eye. But eyesight differences and other camera models often make the right eye the better one for viewing.

Many photographers use "pistol" grips which may be attached to the base of a camera, which is then triggered by a finger of the hand which grips the pistol-type handle. This enhances stability for some, but seems to encourage sloppiness and resulting shakiness for others. Before going to a pistol grip for the B&H 70, be sure this gives steadier shots than the two-handed cradling method described above. The Bolex is

THE BELL & HOWELL 70DR has long been the most used silent camera in television news. It is rugged and dependable, an ideal camera for instructional use. Beth Allen, WAOW-TV, Wausau, Wis., uses the left-eyed viewing and hand-holding position recommended by Bell & Howell. A wide-angle lens is in shooting position in the middle, a 3-inch (telephoto) lens is at the top of the turret, and a 1-inch (standard) lens is at the bottom.

THE BOLEX H-16 is a quiet-running precision camera. Hand-holding is best done with a pistol grip, as demonstrated by Tracy Regan, KWWL-TV, Waterloo, Iowa. Tripod support would be needed for zooming while shooting with the 12-120mm zoom lens.

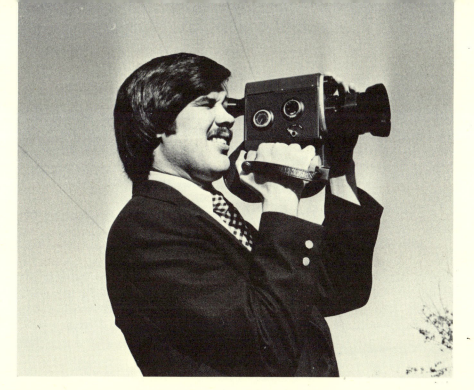

THE CANON SCOOPIC is a compact battery-driven camera which the survey conducted for this book showed to be gaining in popularity. Mark Oppold, WMT-TV, Cedar Rapids, Iowa, uses the hand grip on the right side, leaving his left hand free for further bracing and for operating the 12.5-75mm zoom lens.

designed for pistol grip operation, and the Scoopic has a special hand-grip on the right side near the base.

Your arms should tend to rest easily against the sides of your chest. Avoid pointing elbows out to the side.

Stand with your feet comfortably apart, one a little in front of the other, to whatever extent you stand most stably.

In holding a camera, stay steady but loose. Tensing up or forcing makes for shakiness. And adapt anything we have recommended to your own body or to a different model of camera. The method which is consistently steadiest for you is the one you should use. But give ours a try, since it's the one that works best for most people.

Winding a Camera

To wind the Bell & Howell with the least effort, use shoulder and upper arm effort as much as possible and work the left side against the right. With the left hand strapped in place as for shooting, tilt the camera slightly to the left. Brace the right thumb and its base against the raised winding key and grip the key. Wind with a slight left-shoulder-forward, right-shoulder-back motion in which the camera body moves forward as the winding key moves back. You'll find this method less tiring than using right wrist motion against the key of an unmoving camera. The recommended camera-forward, winding-key-back motion also provides more "wind" per stroke. Don't bother to release the key when returning to starting position for the next stroke of windup, since the key shifts into neutral when moved clockwise.

Wind a camera as you wind a watch—until the instant it balks. Then stop. Don't force it.

After winding, fold the key flat against the side of the camera. Otherwise, it will rotate as the camera runs.

Make a habit of keeping the camera wound. When you have some time after a shot, wind it again. Then when you need to do a lengthy shot or series in fast succession, there's less chance of running down in the middle of a shot. The Bell & Howell has a rated capacity of 22 feet (37 seconds) and the Bolex 18 feet (30 seconds) per winding, but don't count on quite that much. The Scoopic is battery-driven.

Running a Camera

To run a camera, push the *starter button* as you would trigger a still camera or a gun—easing into a sque-e-e-eze that does not move the camera. Squeeze all the way firmly and hold throughout the shot. Then release the button without jolting the camera.

The camera will keep running after the finger is removed if you (a) depress the lock pin just below the starter button of the B&H, (b) set the side release of the Bolex on "M," or (c) turn the Scoopic's shutter button clockwise. To stop the camera before it runs down, the control must be reset. Because these operations usually jolt a hand-held camera, lock mechanisms should be used only with a tripod.

Camera speed—always 24 frames per second (fps) for normal motion on television—is set with a dial located near the top of the B&H and Scoopic cameras and slightly below the center of the Bolex. A range of settings—from 8 to 64 on the B&H, 16-64 on the Scoopic 16M, and 12-64 on the Bolex—is available.

Settings greater than 24 fps give slow motion and those less than 24 fps give fast (speeded up) motion when the film is projected at the 24 fps which is constant for television. If you shoot at the so-called "silent" speed of 16 fps, your film will come over TV like an old Keystone Kops movie.

Before shooting, check to see that the camera speed is set exactly at 24 fps, in case it has been moved. Should you change speeds for deliberate fast or slow motion, be sure to reset at 24 fps to be ready for normal motion again.

The *footage counter* tells how much of the roll of film has been shot. The counter on the B&H must be set manually to indicate the

PARALLAX CAN BE A PROBLEM when viewing is not through the lens. In filming at close range, parallax error can cause you to see a properly composed picture in the viewfinder (left), while the shooting lens, a short distance to the right, is seeing something else.

start of a roll. To move it, you need just the right counter-clockwise touch. Practice until you get the knack. Thumbs or thumb and fore-finger against opposite sides of the counter works for most people. The Bolex and Scoopic have counters that set themselves when the recommended amount of film leader has been run off.

Viewing and Parallax

What you see is what you get with the Scoopic and Bolex, because these cameras have through-the-lens reflex viewing systems. But the lens and viewfinder operate independently on the B&H, and for you to view the same image as the lens requires an adjustment for *parallax,* the lateral difference between the field of the viewfinder and the field of the shooting lens.

The parallax adjustment turns the viewfinder slightly toward or from the lens until their lines of sight intersect at the appropriate dis-tance. Parallax is mainly a problem for subjects up close. A setting of 12 feet is usually good all the way to infinity with a normal focal length lens. But shooting at a distance of 5 feet, for example, requires ad-justing the parallax setting to 5 feet. Otherwise, composition will be off to the right—a door sign may read "lice Chief" with blank space on the right and "Po" lost to parallax.

Reflex viewing permits you to check focus through the lens of the Scoopic or Bolex. But the B&H has only a *critical focuser* which is located below the word "lock." This permits through-the-lens viewing of a tiny portion of the picture to see if it is in focus. However, for the hand-holding which most newsfilm work involves, the tiny bit of picture tends to jump around too much for most photographers to tell much from it.

When shooting without reflex viewing, you must be sure that the viewfinder in position matches the lens. Otherwise, you may compose a shot of two subjects in the 1-inch viewfinder only to discover later that the 3-inch lens was taking the picture, and what it got was a patch of open space between the subjects. If the camera is loaded when you discover that the lens and viewfinder *turrets* of the B&H 70 do not match, you can correct this without opening the camera. Simply unscrew the viewfinder elements and put them in the holes that synchronize with the lenses.

Loading and Unloading

Loading the Bell & Howell is explained in an instruction sheet prepared for beginners at WWBT, Richmond, Va., by Jerry Cardwell and his colleagues:

> Only one side of the camera will open for film to be loaded, the left side. This is the reverse side from the wind key. When the camera is resting on the wind key side and the lens facing forward, two silver circles with a ridge through the center of each are visible. To open the camera, grasp a ridge with each hand and turn toward the center. Then lift up to remove the door.
> The first step in the loading procedure is to locate a small post in the rear center section of the opened camera. Pull this post back as far as possible to open the film gate. Next the unexposed roll of film is placed on the spindle on the right with the film coming off the reel in a clockwise fashion. The film is then placed behind the sprocket drive unit, looped around and placed in the film gate. Take care that the pull-down claw (located in the film gate) engages a sprocket hole to hold the film in place. Loop the film again and place behind the sprocket drive unit on the left side. The film gate is then closed to lock in the film.
> Activate the camera in a short push of the trigger to see if the film is properly threaded. Then wind the film on an empty reel clockwise and place the reel on the empty spindle. Hit the trigger again briefly to make sure that the film is running through the camera properly. Finally, put the door back in place and turn the ridges away from the center to lock it in place.

Loops should be comfortably loose without touching the camera body. A loop that is too tight can jump and jam. One that is too close to the camera body can jump a perforation and rub against the body, which may scratch the delicate film emulsion which records the picture. Bell & Howell recommends 7 perforations in the upper loop and 6 in the lower, with each loop a quarter of an inch from the metal camera body.

Bolex and Scoopic cameras have automatic threading.

After the camera has been closed, run off 4 feet of *leader*. That, added to the 2 feet used in loading and 4 feet to be run off at the end of the roll, accounts for the 10 feet of throwaway film included in 100-foot rolls, which must thus actually total 110 feet.

Next, set the B&H *footage counter* at 0. Or set it at 96 before running off the 4 feet and it will come up on 0. Counters on the Bolex and Scoopic set themselves automatically.

To *unload* at the end of a roll, run the camera until a change in the running noise indicates that the last film has gone through. Once the camera is opened, get the exposed film into a can as fast as possible to prevent light damage.

To unload in the middle of a roll, run off 4 feet of film, open the camera, snap the film where it enters the takeup reel (the one on the left as the B&H points forward), remove that reel and promptly fasten it into a film can. Then, without disturbing the threading, run off about a half foot of film, insert it in the slot of a new takeup reel (always carry a spare!), put the reel on the post, push the trigger for just long enough to be sure the film is running through properly, close the camera and run off 4 feet of leader. The footage counter will need no adjustment.

To guard against film becoming too loosely spooled on a reel, which could let light in, try to keep a finger pressed against the film on any reel being handled in a lighted room.

LOADING THE BELL & HOWELL 70DR.

Practice loading and unloading with an outdated or otherwise useless roll of film until you can do it perfectly every time, even in the dark and on your lap rather than the table top which you won't have under field conditions.

The masking tape which sealed the film can should be wrapped crossways around the can of exposed film and marked with the type of film (7242, etc.) and topic of the story (street repairs, etc.). Do not use cellophane tape. It is too difficult to remove.

If there are any irregularities—such as underexposure or a suspicion that the film may be torn or otherwise damaged—attach a note to so inform the processing lab.

What If It Doesn't Work?

If you push the button and nothing happens, check the camera from the outside first:

—Is the lens in shooting position?
—Is the camera wound?
—Is the camera excessively cold?

If it still is not working, open the camera and check inside:

—Is the film gate arm all the way forward?
—Is the loop okay?
—Are the sprocket holes engaged at all required points?

A balk in the middle of the roll (usually after 20-30 feet of shooting) may mean the film was not engaged in the takeup reel slot and is now jammed messily in the takeup chamber. If you suspect this and the exposed film is valuable, the internal check should be made in the dark. Again, we advise that you learn to load and unload a camera in the dark.

Camera Care

Keep the camera clean, especially around the film gate and pressure plate. Check regularly for dirt or lint. In *cleaning*, never poke around in the film gate area with anything sharp or metallic. A Q-tip type soft swab may be used carefully. The safest technique is to puff your breath through the film gate while the camera is running and the lens has been removed from the turret hole.

In *lubricating* the camera, adapt the manufacturer's recommendations to your situation, especially regarding weather. A heavily oiled camera may run sluggishly or even freeze up when it is very cold. Do *not* over-oil. Wind the camera fully and let it run down a time or two to circulate the oil thoroughly.

Keep a filter holder in the filter slot to prevent light leaks.

USING LENSES

Handle lenses with special care. With a turreted Bell & Howell, rack lenses (go from one to another) into shooting position by handling the turret, NOT by gripping the lenses. Forcing a lens can throw it out of calibration. The Bolex has a fold-away lever for turning its turret. The Scoopic 16M has no turret.

Focal Length

Lenses are classified by focal length, which determines how much they spread out or narrow the view of a scene. The *standard* or normal lens for 16mm cameras, the one giving the least distortion of spatial perspective, is the 1-inch (25mm). A lens shorter in focal length (e.g. 15mm) is called *wide angle*, and a longer one (e.g. 2-inch) is *telephoto.*

The *standard* (1-inch) lens gives perspective most nearly as it [standard] looks to the eye. But one of television's limitations is that a lens view is literally a one-eyed view, and it thus tends to yield a two-dimensional (flat) image in contrast to a person's normal two-eyed (three-dimensional) viewing of reality.

A *wide angle* lens, in covering more area from the same distance, [wide angle] tends to stretch or warp the image, especially around the edges, and thus to add apparent dimension. Distance and speed of movement to or from camera may be distorted. Basketball players coming down court toward an extremely wide angle lens may appear to move at slightly superhuman speed down a long, long floor. As a gimmick, commercials have created grossly enlarged noses on actors simply by moving in close with a very wide angle lens. Such distortion is normally not present with a 15mm lens, but be careful when shooting extreme closeups with a 10mm or 12mm lens. Overall, the spaciousness and dimension which a wide angle lens can add in crowded quarters recommend it for the heavy use it gets in television news.

Another attraction of a wide angle lens is that its depth of field (area of acceptable focus) is greater than for other lenses.

Wide angle lenses are recommended for dim scenes. Not only is depth of field greater, but the most used wide angle lenses are *fast—* they open up to let in a lot of light. For example, a popular 15mm Angenieux opens to f/1.3. But at the other end, this lens and many other wide ones close down only to f/16 and thus may require additional filtering for outdoor shooting.

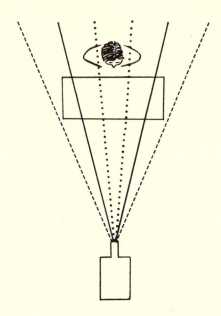

THE ANGLE OF VIEW varies
with the focal length of the lens.
A long (e.g. 2-inch) lens gives a
narrow view (dotted line) and a
wide angle lens gives a broad
view (broken line) relative to
the area shown by a 1-inch lens
(solid line) on a 16mm camera.

telephoto

Whereas a wide angle lens appears to add dimension, a *telephoto* lens such as the 3-inch appears to take it away. It covers less area and flattens the image. Objects not only appear closer, but they move to and from the camera as on a treadmill. In a televised baseball game, a telephoto lens located at the centerfield wall may compress the distance between pitcher and batter for a strange effect. And in a race, as the horses move from the back stretch toward the long telephoto lens, they look as if they are running hard but almost standing still.

A very long telephoto lens following action at a distance can sometimes give an illusion of the camera moving parallel to the subject. This is easiest with a general background such as the sky or a plain, for example, a shot of a tractor moving across a wheat field.

A *zoom* lens differs from others in that its focal length may be varied by the photographer, for example, from 12mm to 120mm. With the turn of a lever or crank for manual or the push of a button for motor-driven zoom lenses, the camera's eye can zoom (change its angle of view) *in* from a wide shot of a political rally to a tight closeup of the speaker, or zoom *out* by going from closeup to wide shot.

zoom

Lens Settings

Two settings must be made on most lenses. One, the aperture or "f" setting, lets in the right amount of light and gives proper *exposure* to the picture. The other, the footage setting, adjusts the lens for the correct distance from the subject and puts the image into *focus*.

Exposure. Much as the iris of the eye contracts in bright sunlight and opens wide in darkness, the *iris diaphragm* of a lens adjusts the size of the opening (*aperture*) which permits light to reach the film. On the Scoopic 16M camera, this adjustment is automatic, battery operated on cue from an electric eye. But on most Bell & Howell and Bolex cameras, the photographer must *"open up"* the lens aperture to let in more light as scenes get dimmer and *"close down"* to admit less light as they become brighter. This is done manually by adjusting the f/stops on the lens, with higher numbered f/stops letting in less light. The most familiar stops are 1.4, 2, 2.8, 4, 5.6, 8, 11, 16 and 22. Closing down by one f/stop (as in going from f/4 to f/5.6) reduces the aperture opening by half, and opening up by one (as in going from f/4 to f/2.8) doubles it.

Most cameras with *automatic exposure control* have an override which permits f/stops to be set manually. However, at WDAY-TV, Fargo, N.D., News Director Norm Schrader says his newsfilm reporters seldom go manual with their Scoopics. About the only time they override automatic exposure control is on a bright day when the only background to a subject is sky, and that calls for opening up roughly half an f/stop more than the metering system says. In most other situations, however, since TV transmission is intolerant of high contrast and is usually set to balance it out automatically through a shading mechanism, Schrader notes, little is lost in letting the electric eye do the job at the time of filming.

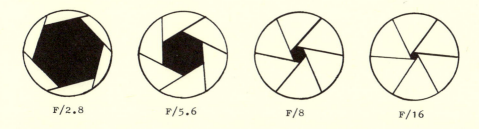

F/2.8   F/5.6   F/8   F/16

THE LENS APERTURE grows smaller, letting in less light, as a higher numbered f/stop is used.

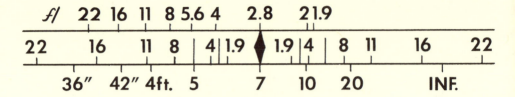

DEPTH OF FIELD is indicated on most lenses by two diverging scales of f/stops located between the scales on which the aperture (upper f/stop scale) and distance (lower scale) are set. If a typical 1-inch lens is set for f/2.8 (upper) and 7 feet (lower), the 2.8 lines on the depth-of-field scale in the middle point down to the nearest and farthest distances of acceptable focus. In this case, depth of field is about 6 to 9 feet from the camera.

Focus. The other lens setting is for focus. It is related to the aperture setting, since opening up to let in more light reduces the *depth of field*—the range of distance from the camera within which subjects will be in acceptable focus. For example, with a Bell & Howell 1-inch lens set for focus at 7 feet, and the aperture set at f/8, the picture should be in focus from 4½ feet to 19 feet. But opening to f/2.8 reduces depth of field to a 6-9 foot range. The example roughly describes the difference between shooting with photo lights and natural light in the typical office, and explains why it is not always easy to get a sharp picture when using existing light indoors.

The closer the camera to the subject, the more difficult the focus. Depth of field is greater behind the point for which focus is set than in front of that point. Depth of field may be checked on most lenses by looking at a special set of f/stop markings which go off in opposite directions from the pointer for the distance-setting. They are located just across the ring from the distance-setting scale. Using the above example, if the settings are 7 feet and f/8, then the 8 on the depth-of-field scale to the left of the footage pointer will be directly across from 4½ feet and the 8 marking to the right will be across from 19 feet.

For maximum sharpness of two objects which are different distances from the camera, keep in mind that the closer you get, the less the depth of field. So don't set the lens for halfway between the objects. Instead, set it about a third of the way back of the near object. For example, the speaker is 12 feet from you but the chart to which he keeps referring is 18 feet. Set the focus at 14 feet, and check to see if both are in focus.

A tape measure is helpful in focusing on very close work. Measure from the *film plane,* which is just back of the lens base and marked with an ϕ on most camera bodies. Light rays focus at the film plane, not at the front of the lens. For example, shooting at f/2.8 and 15 inches, the picture would be in focus if the 15 inches was measured from the film plane but probably out if measured from the front of the lens.

For TV, there is no in-between. If a subject is soft or just a little fuzzy, it is out of focus. And it's better to have a background all the way out of focus than just soft enough to annoy the viewer who is trying to comprehend it.

Though depth of field increases with higher f/stop numbers, sharpness of overall picture does so only within limits. Some lenses are sharpest when just a bit short of being closed down all the way. Though the "diffraction" which may occur from closing a lens all the way is usually indiscernible, some photographers feel more comfortable with f/16 than with the maximum f/22 on a lens.

In focusing a reflex lens, keep in mind that the wider open the lens, the less the depth of field. Thus the sharpest through-the-lens focusing is to be had by setting the distance when the aperture is wide open and then closing down to the appropriate f/stop. This is usually necessary only in situations where depth of field is very limited. Caution: After focusing, don't leave the lens wide open unless that is the correct f/stop.

In focusing a zoom lens, the rules for reflex viewing apply, as does the rule that depth of field is more of a problem at the telephoto setting. Set the lens for distance while viewing at the telephoto rather than wide angle focal lengh. Otherwise, the sharp wide scene may turn soft when you zoom in for the telephoto closeup.

Lens Care

Lenses are delicate. A jet of air from a rubber ear syringe is sometimes recommended for removing dust. Breath plus an easy rub with photographic lens-cleaning paper may also be used. But don't use regular eyeglass-cleaning paper, as most of it is coated with silicone, which is too abrasive for most lens surfaces. The care that must be taken in cleaning lenses is summarized by Fred Brooks, news director at WBRZ-TV, Baton Rouge, La.:

> The lenses in use today are "coated" with a substance that makes them more than an ordinary piece of ground glass. This coating, commonly referred to as "color coating," can be damaged by improper cleaning of the lens. Do not—I repeat, DO NOT—clean a lens with any material other than a standard lens tissue or other very soft substance. Even then, it is desirable to "breathe" on the lens to moisten it slightly, and wipe very carefully. Begin at the center and in circular motions wipe to the outside of the element. If the lens coating is damaged, it can cause light rays to enter the camera incorrectly and spoil the picture.

REMINDERS

- Get to know the camera before going out to shoot.
- Practice loading until you can do it perfectly every time, even in the dark.
- Double-check the viewfinder position and fps setting.
- Check parallax, especially for closeups.
- Shoot from a comfortable but steady position.
- Ease into the starter button "sque-e-e-e-eze."
- Keep the camera wound between shots.
- Lens focal length is wide angle, standard (1-inch for 16mm film) and telephoto.
- The higher the f/stop, the less light hits the film.
- Focusing becomes easier with 1) a wider angle lens, 2) a higher f/stop and 3) greater distance from the subject.
- Wide angle lenses are popular because of their 1) wide view in crowded quarters, 2) added "dimension," 3) greater depth of field and 4) low-light capability (for the most-used models).
- Keep the camera and lenses clean.

3 | Lens View of Reality

Think of the camera as an eye, a proxy for the eyes of the home viewer. Your job as a camera reporter is to "see" for the members of the audience, to show them the reality of news events and situations. You are not a filmmaker taking liberties with reality for the sake of an art. You are a journalist whose first rule is accuracy as you use the tools of newsfilm to make the home viewer an eyewitness to reality.

This means using the camera to show things in the natural ways people look at them. Your prime responsibility in shooting newsfilm is to provide the viewer with a realistic experience. This basic rule underlies other guidelines for composition, continuity and story-telling.

A STEADY VIEW

As an eyewitness to reality, the viewer deserves a steady view, not the nervous antics of a pan-happy, zoom-happy or shaky newsfilm photographer. Unnecessary camera or lens movement is the single most common problem of beginners. As noted by Wayne Vriesman, news director, KWGN-TV, Denver:

> An amateur cameramen is easy to spot. He usually commits two basic sins: He *pans*, that is, moves the camera. And he *shakes*. For some reason, an amateur believes that since it's a movie camera, it's supposed to move. Not so. If anything moves, it's the subject, the object you are filming. If it does move, and you want to follow it, OK. But unless you are a real professional, a good rule to follow is *don't pan*. And *hold that camera steady*. A shaking camera makes a viewer seasick.

35

Steadiness

Most people are not as steady as they think they are. The idea solution is to mount the camera on a tripod. But this is often ruled out by the fast pace and mobility required in shooting newsfilm. Silent cameras can be hand-held effectively for most news work. But if a sound-on-film camera is not supported by a tripod, the hands need steadying help from a body brace or shoulder pod.

When shakiness is a problem, the following can help you get steadier shots:

1) *Use all available bracing,* including your body. In hand-holding a camera, steady it with both hands when possible, elbows tucked lightly into the body, feet spread slightly apart with one a bit in front of the other. Avoid unnecessary breathing or other body movement during a hand-held shot. It can also help if you brace yourself against a relatively fixed object such as a wall, fence post or your automobile.

2) *Use a wider angle lens.* Camera motion shows up more as lens focal length increases. Shakiness that is imperceptible with a 10mm lens can make an old salt seasick when seen through a 75mm lens.

3) *Avoid motionless subjects* as much as is practical. Camera motion shows up more when a subject is stationary, as a sign or a speaker at the podium, then when it is moving. For example, basketball and other fast-moving sports can be shot with a hand-held telephoto lens, because attention is on the movement and few people notice the shaking of the ever-changing background. But a hand-held telephoto shot of a golfer putting will probably be too shaky. Shakiness may go unnoticed if the background is sky or water, but not if it is a building.

Steadiness is particularly important in film shot without a tripod if it is to be edited in to adjoin tripod-supported film. Visual continuity is jolted, for example, in cutting from a steady shot of a speaker to a shaky shot of the audience, as often happens when a speaker is filmed with a tripod-supported sound camera and crowd shots are taken with a hand-held silent camera.

Panning

Turning the camera from one position to another while shooting is known as panning. The term derives from the use of camera movement to provide a "panoramic" view of a scene. Unfortunately, beginners tend to pan so much that some news directors instruct them not to pan at all. That may be a bit extreme. A slow, steady pan can serve a purpose—as showing the extent of tornado devastation or the scope of a building project. More often than not, however, two or more shots from different angles with the camera held without movement will do the job better. Before panning, be sure the pan is necessary. Usually it is not.

If panning, do it right.

In using a tripod, practice until you develop smooth, steady control of the handle. To avoid jerky starts, ease into a pan just as you ease into the triggering of a camera.

In hand-held, body-braced or shoulder-podded shooting, plan your body movement in advance, when possible, to wind up in your most comfortable and controlled position. Plant yourself facing the direction in which the pan will end. Then, moving only the upper body, you can turn back to the beginning position, start the shot, pan, and hold the final seconds of the film more steadily than if your body were turning into the less comfortable position.

Avoid beginning or ending shots in the middle of pans. Hold the shot still for a moment, pan, then hold briefly again. In a few cases you may cut from one shot to another of unbroken movement in the same direction—as with consecutive moving aerials of a forest.

Pan stationary scenes slowly and steadily, allowing the viewer time to take in significant detail.

A swish pan moves quickly from one point to the other, deliberately swishing out details along the way. If unable to get a sign and the build- ing it identifies into the frame at the same time, you might swish pan from one to the other. But use this technique sparingly.

Never pan back and forth—an amateur act known as "spraying the garden."

Turning the camera *to follow action* should be distinguished from other forms of panning in that the main subject is not actually being panned. As the camera turns to follow a fire truck, a motorcade or basketball action, it is the relatively low-interest background which is being panned, not the action which is the center of attention. In- cidentally, a good rule in shooting sports is always to follow the ball.

In following action, *lead* it slightly, by leaving a little more space on the side of the frame in the direction of movement. This gives a natural effect and helps keep the action from getting away from you. The ball, for example, is less likely to go out of frame if you are lead- ing it.

We repeat—pan sparingly. Pans to follow a moving object are usually permissible. But pans for other purposes—such as showing area, especially closeup—are often ineffective and indicative of a lazy, un- imaginative photographer. Two or more stationary shots of a building or a crowd taken from different angles will usually show it better than a pan from one side to the other. Such pans are anathema to the editor who wants to shorten the shots, and they lead news directors like Wayne Vriesman (KWGN-TV, Denver) and Jim Marshall (WBAY-TV, Green Bay) to say the safest general advice for a beginner is— don't pan.

Zooming

The same amateur who pans too much also tends to run a zoom lens in and out as if playing a trombone. The television viewer, intent on the alternately growing and shrinking picture, soon develops the feeling of being on the end of a yo-yo string.

Like the camera, the zoom lens is best thought of as a device to record movement rather than to create it. It is generally best used, not for zooming while shooting, but as a lens with an infinite number of focal lengths with the proper length to be selected for each shot.

Zoom while shooting only to help tell the story. It is, of course, effective to zoom in on the outfielder going back for a catch, or to zoom out from a closeup of a speaker to show the context of a large crowd. In a hectic situation, zooming may be preferable to stopping the camera, resetting the lens and perhaps missing some crucial action. Similarly, zooming may be used to good advantage in shooting "standup" film, in which the reporter is seen (usually standing) telling a story at the scene of the news event. Zooming in can concentrate attention on the reporter's remarks without breaking continuity as might be the case in abruptly cutting from a wide shot of the scene to a closeup of the reporter.

Dollying

Whereas a zoom only makes it look as though you are moving in or out on a subject, a dolly involves actually doing it. In Hollywood movies, cameras are placed on wheeled devices called dollies to move toward, from, or parallel with an object or action. This is not practical on most news stories. But, with practice, you should be able to do a reasonably smooth walking dolly, either with a hand-held silent camera or a shoulder-podded or body-braced sound camera. Such shooting while walking requires that you develop a gyroscopic sense of camera-balance. It's easier when moving in on or among moving objects than when moving in on a fixed object such as a sign. Shooting from a moving vehicle can also give a dolly effect. As with panning and zooming, use the dolly in moderation and only for a purpose.

COMPOSITION

Good composition results from a sense of the visual which you must develop on an individual basis. Relying too much upon a set of rules can make your work mechanical and monotonous, while perhaps technically correct. Some of the best newsfilm photographers have never heard of "the rule of thirds" or others to be found in the literature on visual communication. They have simply developed an awareness of how visual elements go together. While in part innate, this awareness can be nourished by watching good film like that in many network newsfilm stories and documentaries. Viewing camera work of the kind Jim Wilson, Izzy Bleckman and others have done for the CBS "On the Road" reports may help you more than any book of visual rules.

Nevertheless, a familiarity with a few of the key elements of visual communication may also help you further develop *your own* sense of ways to "see" effectively for your newsfilm audience.

Visual Structure and Framing

Composition is formed by determining the visual *point of interest*, which is the key point to which you want the viewer's eye to gravitate, and then building around this point.

The *rule of thirds* says that, given a normal picture, the eye tends to gravitate to a point one-third from the left or right side and one-third from top or bottom. This places the center of attention somewhat away from the center of the frame. Notice the composition on television news programs. Newscasters and others who are seen talking are often not centered in the frame. A variety of composition is used, including occasional perfectly centered shots. But very often, consciously or unconsciously, what roughly amounts to the rule of thirds is observed.

Framing should direct attention to the central object. Shooting through a doorway and showing part of the door frame can make it clear that you are moving into a room. And *lines* can help. A line leading into the picture from one edge tends to draw the viewer's eye with it.

Lines may also add *perspective*, as with railroad tracks or airport runways leading off into the distance. Such lines help add a third dimension to a medium which is restricted by its size and format on the home screen.

Relative *size* is a key element of perspective. Nothing communicates how big an object is as well as showing a small object next to it, as a sub-compact car beside a semi-trailer truck. Abstract sizes become concrete when *people* are shown with them. A new building may look like an architect's model unless people are shown moving around in the scene.

Psychological distance can also be suggested to some extent by composition. The closer together two persons are shown, the more they seem attracted to each other. The farther apart, the more repelled. A shot of two political opponents may be visually most consistent with reality if you put some screen distance between them.

Lines also tend to have certain connotations. *Horizontal* lines are restful, *vertical* lines indicate strength, and *jagged* lines suggest action.

Nicely balanced framing tends to be *restful,* and too much of it is boring. On the other hand, composition which is irregular, complex or unstable may be *stressful,* and sometimes that is the mood a scene should convey.

Angles may also carry psychological implications. An interview, for example, should normally be shot with the camera at *eye level.* From the viewer's perspective, looking down on an interviewee tends to downgrade or belittle. The reverse applies to a low angle. Looking up at someone makes the person appear powerful and perhaps cold and impersonal.

Shooting at an angle usually adds dimension. Head-on shots tend to be flat and often unflattering of subjects.

Slight angles are usually more effective than extreme ones, and unusual angles should be used sparingly. Beginners tend to be led astray by angular new ways of seeing things. Everyone has seen at least one feature story filmed "as seen through the eye of . . ." The approach is a novelty that wears thin quickly. Departing from the normal way of "seeing" things put the viewer to work trying to relate to an unfamiliar point of view. This should be held to a minimum and used only when it helps tell the story. A scene can usually be shot from many angles, but only a few are physically logical in that they represent possible angles the home viewer might use if present at the event. Vary your angles, but don't overdo them, and always keep them logical.

Back up to frame a little more area than you want to go out on the air. This compensates for *oversweep,* the electronic scanning which crops off about a tenth of the picture around the edges, in transmission. This is the border that most home viewers never see. In general, it's better to shoot a little too wide than too tight.

Foreground objects can add dimension. For example, part of a tree or fence in the foreground can help put a building in perspective. But don't strain for cute framing. Those shots through tree boughs can easily look contrived. And some foreground objects—wastebaskets, handbags and such—are usually to be avoided in that they only clutter and distract.

OVERSWEEP is the picture area around the edges of the frame which is often lost in TV projection and transmission.

Backgrounds should also be either neutral or germane to the story. For a standup report, the background should normally be part of the story. In general for most newsfilm, the simpler the background, the more attention will be concentrated on the subject. Bright flowered wallpaper competes with a face, and a light stand or clothes tree "growing out" of a subject's head distracts.

Plain dark backgrounds may swallow up people or objects in front of them. When the head of an interviewee appears disembodied on a dark blue backdrop, this is probably a result of a close match between suit color and wall color. On the other hand, too light a background may—through electronic shading in transmission—make the subject's face so dark as to be unrecognizable.

Finally, try to keep camera showoffs out of your backgrounds. Someone smiling, winking or waving at the audience is extremely distracting.

Lens Selection

Choosing a lens involves a compositional decision. You may think many elements of the scene are important and choose a wide angle lens. Or you may decide to concentrate on a smaller area, making each element relatively more important, and work with a 1-inch or telephoto lens. In effect, you compose by adding or subtracting picture elements.

As noted in Chapter 2, focal length other than the standard *1-inch* for 16mm film may distort perspective by appearing to add breadth and depth to the scene with a wide angle or to flatten it with a telephoto lens.

While the "dimension" added by a *wide angle* lens usually helps the unnaturally flat TV picture, it may also distort the reality you are trying to report. Small rooms look more spacious through a wide angle lens. Such distortion may be irrelevant for an office interview of an official, but not for a story on crowded tenements.

With a *telephoto* lens, the apparently compressed image can be used for such effects as "stacking" cars in a traffic jam. But remember that such distortion is not reality. The telephoto lens should be used sparingly for such special effects. Its primary purpose is to enable a usable picture at a distance too great for a standard lens.

CONTINUITY

The essence of telling a newsfilm story is continuity—how the shots fit together sequentially. The film story should flow smoothly from one shot or sequence to the next. As described by KWGN-TV's Wayne Vriesman:

> Continuity . . . means, of course, the film *flows*. It visually has a beginning, a middle and an ending. Ideally, the film is telling the complete story . . . and ideally, the film should not require a script because the cameraman is doing his job. This all takes planning. Your first shot is an establisher so you know where a particular event is occurring. You switch logically from one scene to the next so the viewer doesn't lose the thread of the story. One shot out of place could throw the viewer completely off course. Heavy action in a film story will be told in one or more sequences, a series of shots arranged logically to give the impression of a complete action, without the time-consuming monotony of a single shot. A riot may last eight hours, but newsfilm squeezes that eight hours into probably no more than three or four minutes.

When the beginning, middle or end of a story is missing or poorly handled, communication suffers. If a story is not adequately established, the viewer spends several seconds (or even the whole story) trying to identify the location or persons involved. Without logical sequences in the middle, not much story is likely to get across. And on some stories, a re-establishing shot is needed at the end to prevent too abrupt a finish.

Establishers

An establisher is the opening shot or sequence of shots in a film story. It sets the stage, establishing location, time, principal subjects and such.

The most used and usually most appropriate establisher is a wide shot which gives the viewer a point of reference—such as a familiar building or a street intersection. A 5-second establisher may carry more information than several paragraphs of newspaper copy, and therein lies a hazard. As much as possible, restrict the scene to essential information. The viewer who becomes fascinated by some irrelevant detail in the corner of the picture may miss the main point. And give the viewer time to digest the information in a scene before piling on new visual information from the next scene.

Variety can be added by occasionally opening a story with a tight closeup, for example, of a convention badge, the drum in a parade's marching band or a spectacular blast of fireworks on July 4. Such attention-getters should normally be run long enough for the viewer to become oriented and should not be overburdened with narration. Let the shot carry itself, either silent or preferably with natural sound, to permit this orientation. Then the viewer, through your camera, can back off and look at the wider scene which would normally be the establisher. But use this technique sparingly. It can easily be overworked.

Beginners tend to overuse closeups of signs as establishers. A sign by itself is not usually a very good opening shot. However, you may get a good effect with a sign in the foreground and a building or action in the background. Especially if the sign is not easily read in this wide shot, a second shot may well be a closeup of the sign.

Sequences

For years, newsfilm editors have preached the *long* shot (LS), *medium* shot (MS) and *closeup* (CU) sequential progression from the establisher into the heart of the story, and for good reason. It draws the viewer along easily and allows natural orientation. It is as if you were walking into the story. First you see the full auditorium from the rear (LS), then you concentrate on the speaker's stand (MS), and finally you look closely at the speaker (CU).

LS, MS and CU indicate perspective rather than absolute distance. For example, long shots may be filmed from 500 feet for a house, 20 feet for a classroom or 5 feet for an architect's model of a building. Medium and closeup shots would be proportional in each case.

Action sequences are series of shots arranged to give the *impression of complete actions*. Impression is an important term, because in reality you seldom record one complete action from beginning to end. A sequence is usually built from pieces of several repeated actions to simulate a single action.

In a construction film, the single action of hooking cable to an I-beam, raising it three stories and bolting the beam in place may take

20 times the 30 seconds the story will be allotted on the air. Yet a single 30-second shot of that beam inching up the side of the building would probably be dull, and would not really tell the story of construction. Several shots of different steps in the action, tied together with editorial devices to be discussed later, will, in effect, compress the action into the available time.

Within the same story, an entirely different sequence may be developed around the work of carpenters on the interior of the building: hauling in lumber, measuring and cutting it, and nailing it in place. On film, a 30-minute process becomes 30 seconds of progressive action tied together in *compressed time.*

In going from one shot to the next, avoid slight changes in angle or distance which would produce a *jump cut*—in which the subject appears to jump a bit closer or shift body angle abruptly from one shot to the next. Moving from a 6-foot to a 4-foot shot or a couple of feet to the side on the 6-foot shot will do this, unless you change to a lens of clearly different focal length. Successive shots of the same subject with the same lens from roughly the same camera locale will almost invariably give a jump cut.

If the camera stops before you finish a shot, don't just start up again or there will be a jump cut. If there is enough to salvage from the first shot, turn the camera and shoot something else related, then go back to a second shot of the original scene. If the first take is too short to use, cover the lens and hit the starter button for a split second of dark film to call the editor's attention to the bad shot.

Don't feel that you must follow the LS, MS, CU sequence rigidly. It has utility in most situations, but many variations are possible. Use the sequences which best tell the story.

Re-establishers

Newsfilm photographers sometimes forget that many stories need re-establishing at the end, getting the viewer out of the story as well as into it. One way is to retrace your steps, "backing out" of it, in effect. The final shot may re-establish the setting. For visual variety, strive for a different but equally effective location shot, or at least a different angle on the one with which you began. The re-establisher concludes the story with no loose ends.

A closeup is sometimes an ideal ending for a story. For example, a closeup of a mother watching firemen drag a river for her missing son sums up the story better than any commentary or wide shot of the scene. Her grief is hers alone. It is not part of the activity at the river, yet it is the point of the whole story. Don't dilute its emotional impact with a wide shot.

EDITORIAL DEVICES

Continuity can be enhanced by techniques called "editorial devices" because they involve editing, either while shooting or later. These techniques, which enable the photographer or editor to compress time and cover rough spots in film, include: 1) the *cutaway*, 2) the *cut-in* and 3) *in-and-out-of-frame*.

Cutaway

The most common editorial device is the cutaway—a scene related to, but not a part of, the main action of the story. We cut from a parade to a child watching from a father's shoulders. We see a closeup of the fire chief between two shots of roaring flames. Or the scoreboard between shots of basketball action.

Jump cuts can be avoided by inserting cutaways between similar shots of speakers, interviewees and other subjects.

Cutaways should be shot with the same care as scenes of the main action. Do not shoot cutaways which are in bad taste or otherwise inappropriate. The home viewer should never see a show-off's obscene gesture between parade shots or an audience laughing between two serious sound film segments of a speech.

Cutaways should be more than devices for smooth editing. They should add to the story. On-air film time is too precious to throw away.

Cut-in

Whereas a cutaway literally cuts away from the main action, a cut-in is part of that action. By changing lenses or positions, you "cut into" the action for a closer look at a detail seen from a distance in the preceding shot. You may cut from a wide shot of a groundbreaking ceremony to a closeup of a shovel turning dirt. Such action should match. If the wide shot ends with feet pushing down on the shovel blade, the cut-in must begin in roughly the same way. A change in camera angle can make changes in position by the subject less noticeable.

Cut-ins advance the story through time and are thus an integral part of sequence development. It may take a fireman 20 seconds to climb a ladder, but in a 3-second scene of his starting up, a 2-second cut-in of his foot on a rung, and a 3-second shot of his reaching the top, you can move him the full distance in 8 seconds. This is not disconcerting to the viewer, who knows the fireman is going all the way to the top and expects him to get there.

THE OVERALL SCENE gives a general impression.

THE CUT-IN concentrates on significant detail, from a slightly different angle but without disorienting the viewer.

THE CUTAWAY, on the other hand, is related to but not part of the main action or scene.

In-and-Out-of-Frame

Perhaps the easiest way to get subjects into and out of film is to let them do it themselves, but this takes planning on your part. The photographer who produces the worst editing problems is the one who "locks on" to a moving subject and follows it relentlessly with the lens. This provides no logical break in the action and demands a cutaway for any shortening.

You can let movement come into or go out of the frame. There is no more logical transition, and all it requires is a little anticipation of the movement. A woman walking out of one frame and into the next obviates the need for any cutaway or cut-in. She removes herself from one scene and appears logically in the next, with no special transitional shot needed. When she moves from one room (and frame) to another, for example, her disappearance and reappearance are accepted without question.

The technique may be used in fast-breaking spot events. KWGN-TV's Wayne Vriesman gives this example:

> Put yourself at a roaring fire. You shoot a fire truck approaching the scene. Your film shows it a half block away traveling about 10 miles an hour. By the time you get to that truck, it's in a stopped position and the firemen are rapidly unloading hose and other equipment. Now, you can't show that fire truck traveling 10 miles an hour, then in the very next scene show it stopped and the firemen unloading it. Again, you are going to jar the viewer. Trucks and men just don't move that fast in reality. So, what do you do? In your first shot, while the truck is approaching, you let it travel out of your frame. In other words, you don't follow the action with your camera. Hold that camera stationary and let the truck drive right out of your picture. Then, after the truck has passed and other action fills the scene, you cut to the men unloading the truck. The eye accepts the disappearance of the truck and then its reappearance, without question.

Keep screen direction in mind. You would not want to show the fire truck leaving the frame at the right in one scene and entering it from the right in the next one. This would look as if it had turned around and was heading back to the station.

SCREEN DIRECTION

There are three directions of real or implied movement on the television screen: *left to right, right to left,* and *neutral* (directly into or away from the camera). Normally, you should choose one of those directions and stay with it throughout the story. Violations of screen direction can be avoided by imagining a *line* through the overall scene —a logical division according to the direction of movement in it—and then shooting from only one side of this line.

Real Movement

With real movement, such as a parade or military review, the rule is simple. *Keep everything moving in the same direction.* If you are filming from the south side of the street with the parade moving from your left to your right, stay there. Do without that shot of the majorette which you could get only from the north side, because on your film she would be marching from right to left, heading for a collision with the band behind her.

There is a way to change screen direction without jolting the viewer. En route to the other side of the street, shoot some film of the band approaching head-on. This is a *neutral* direction, and it provides a weak but acceptable transition when you must change sides.

In short, either keep the action moving in one direction or use a neutral shot to take the viewer with you in changing directions.

It may help to notice the center line of the parade street. To keep screen direction constant, choose one side of that line and stay on it—unless you ease the viewer to the other side.

Implied Movement

With implied movement, no one will paint a line for you. It must be imagined. Implied movement means that the action is relatively static, but a form of movement takes place in an exchange of some kind. For example, we may move back and forth between shots of interviewer and interviewee or between speaker and audience.

This exchange, this movement of view back and forth between people, establishes a line—a 180 degree area to which the camera is restricted—as surely as does a parade. You usually have a choice of which side of the line to shoot from. But once you have chosen a side, stick to it.

Interview Shots. The problem is exemplified in a typical interview situation—one interviewer, one interviewee. They talk to each other, not directly to the camera. The line thus established runs between and through the two people. Though the camera will normally be set up to shoot the interviewee nearly full face, this person will still be looking, however slightly, either to the left or right of the screen, in the direction of the interviewer. Logically then, cutaway or reversal shots should show the interviewer looking in the opposite direction, at the interviewee.

This is especially important in shooting sound reversals—full shots of the interviewer asking the question, usually shot as re-asks after the actual interview. Make a note of the interviewee's screen direction, then set up the interviewer in the opposite direction for the reversals. If both persons face the same way on the home screen, it looks as if one is talking to the back of the other's head.

Speech Shots. The same principles apply in shooting a speech. The line runs between the speaker and the audience. Ideally the photographer sets up between the speaker and the line of seats closest to a side wall of the auditorium. This is not always physically possible. Look for other ways to keep the viewer oriented. For example, a wide shot showing both speaker and audience can help maintain perspective.

REVERSAL CUTAWAYS of an interview must observe the rules of screen direction. In this University of Wisconsin lab demonstration, Bob Crider's sound-on-film will show Prof. James Hoyt looking to the left of the screen. Thus Tracy Regan's silent cutaways must show interviewer Tom Beell looking to the right. All filming is done from the same side of an imaginary line running between and through the interviewer and the interviewee.

Action Effects

If smooth one-way direction reduces confusion, it follows that the mood of a confused event may be enhanced by changes of screen direction. Especially in film of forceful action, *intercutting* scenes with changing screen direction helps communicate the confusion or excitement of the event—for example, a mob action, a victory celebration or a rock festival.

A change in screen direction repeated over and over can produce tension in the viewer. In filming a police line confronting advancing demonstrators, cutting back and forth between demonstrators moving to the left and police facing right is consistent with the tenseness of the situation.

Screen direction can sometimes be changed without either a neutral shot or confusion. Using a *match-reverse*, the camera follows an action in one direction until it meets an action going the opposite direction and follows the second action back the other way. This can be done in filming a fashion show, for example. With more than one model parading at one time, follow one until another model is met going the other way, then follow the second one back the other way.

CAMERA SPEED

If all television newsfilm runs on the air at 24 *frames per second,* why did they put those other speeds on the camera? There are appropriate uses of slow and fast motion, the mechanics of which are explained in Chapter 2. But any variation from 24 fps is a distortion of reality and must be used with discretion.

Distortion for Effect

Sports of all kinds provide opportunities for occasional slow motion photography. The frantic activity of the football field can be slowed down to let the viewer better appreciate the coordination and skill of a runner. Since it is apparent to any viewer that the motion is slower than real, no deception is involved. However, motion just slightly off can fool the viewer. Shooting sports action at 30 fps to extend it a bit, as is often done for basketball, tends to show the details of the game better. While this may perhaps be justified on those grounds, keep in mind that such film does not show the real ball game but one which has been slowed down photographically.

Similarly, traffic can be made to appear moving at a higher speed, without apparent distortion, by shooting it at 16 fps. But ask yourself— is this the honest portrayal of reality which the viewer has a right to expect from television news?

Conspicuous fast motion can be comic, but not everyone has the same sense of humor. And in a standard situation such as children getting out of school for summer vacation, it tends to be a cliché.

To East the Bumps

A valid use of slow motion is to reduce the bounce in aerial photography. Sharp bumping, if shot at 64 fps, becomes gentle floating when the film is projected at 24 fps. The same applies to shooting from a moving car. If the pavement is relatively smooth, filming from a car can be done at 48 to 32 fps without undue jerkiness.

Keep in mind the time factor. An aerial scene shot at 64 fps will take 2 2/3 as long to run on the air as it did to shoot. Your 100 feet of film will run off at the faster rate too.

To Prolong a Scene

Slow motion can string out a film story which you do not have as long to shoot as you would like. For example, a prisoner is to be whisked from a car into the courthouse in what should be about a 10-second walk. By shooting at a faster camera speed, you can stretch this into 20-30 seconds. Of course, the prisoner will look knee-deep in molasses. This is a point at which editorial judgment enters. Is it better to show 10 normal-action seconds, with the possibility of freezing a frame of the film and holding it if it is that important, or to go ahead and show 20-30 seconds of obviously distorted movement?

Extra F/Stops

Slow or fast camera speeds may be used to slow down or increase shutter speeds for the purpose of increasing or decreasing the amount of light hitting the film.

For example, a lens may open to only f/1.4 but the exposure meter says an additional f/stop is needed for a long shot of the audience in a dim auditorium. By shooting at 12 fps instead of 24, you can pick up that extra f/stop's worth of light. Just be sure to do this when everyone is sitting still, because any motion will come on the home screen at twice normal speed. That includes your body motion, so try to brace the camera against a fixed object for such shooting.

Similarly, you may find yourself shooting a story that's all indoors except for a long establishing shot of the building's exterior. The lens will close down to only f/16 but the meter says shoot at f/22. Shooting at 48 fps will keep out that extra f/stop of light. Steadiness will be no problem this time, but remember that any movement in the picture will be conspicuously in slow motion.

For typical TV newsfilm ASA ratings, changing camera speed will affect exposure roughly as follows:

64 fps—You lose 1⅓ f/stops.
48 fps—You lose 1 f/stop.
32 fps—You lose ½ f/stop.
24 fps—Normal.
16 fps—You gain ½ f/stop.
12 fps—You gain 1 f/stop.
 8 fps—You gain 1½ f/stops.

EDITING IN CAMERA

Awareness of continuity and other principles discussed in this chapter can help you to edit in camera, a practice encouraged at most stations. This means, to the extent practical, shooting the story the way you think it should appear on the air. There are good reasons for this:

VISUALIZING SHOTS in their story context before shooting them is important for effective in-camera editing. Carol Norton was a graduate teaching assistant in broadcast journalism at the University of Wisconsin when this photo was made.

1) It *saves film*. Editing in camera usually gets a story shot with less footage than the helter-skelter approach of shooting in no particular order.

2) It forces *story planning* and indicates a camera reporter rather than just a picture shooter. By so planning, you may include a vital shot which otherwise might not have come to mind.

3) It *saves time*. This is the main reason for editing in camera. Deadlines get tight in TV newsrooms late in the day, and any saving of editing-bench time puts you that much ahead.

4) *Fewer splices* mean stronger film. Most hot splicers do a good job, but spliced film is still more likely to break than unspliced film.

Editing in camera requires that you shoot in logical sequences, keep adjoining shots compatible, and hold down the footage. You must plan shots, knowing what you want before you push the starter button. It is not uncommon for pros to shoot stories that can go on the air without one change at the editing table. They have learned to use the camera as a tool of reporting.

Some stories lend themselves to more in-camera editing than others. Silent film of a housing project or turkey farm may well be planned and edited entirely in the camera. Silent footage of fires, accident scenes and other spot news often requires little editing. Sound film nearly always must be edited back at the station. And a visually complex story in which scenes must be made to fit a reporter's script permits relatively little of the editing to be done in-camera. For any story, cutaways and other editorial devices may be shot out of sequence, through convenience or necessity. The typical story will require some editing. But the less the better—especially when the hands on the clock are edging close to newscast time.

REMINDERS

- Show things in the natural way people look at them.
- Avoid panning, except to follow a moving object. Panning is usually not the best way to show area.
- Avoid excessive zooming.
- Normally, do not begin or end a shot in the middle of a pan or zoom.
- Steadiness is enhanced by 1) using all available bracing, 2) using a wider angle lens and 3) avoiding motionless subjects.
- In composing, determine the point of interest and build around this point, being aware of lines, angles and other elements of visual structure.
- The center of attention is usually best placed away from the center of the frame.
- Shoot wide enough to allow for picture-edge loss in transmission.
- Try to frame out distracting elements.
- Every story should have a beginning, middle and end.
- Most stories are best established with a wide shot.
- The most used sequence of shots goes from long (LS) to medium (MS) to closeup (CU) of a subject.
- Consecutive shots of a subject with the same lens from roughly the same angle and distance will give a jump cut.
- Shoot plenty of cutaways.
- Normally, shoot from only one side of movement such as in a parade or basketball game.
- Use fast-motion and slow-motion sparingly. They distort reality.
- In-camera editing saves film, splices and time.

4 | Film and Lighting

Film is comparable to the retina of the eye. Like optic nerve ends, film's light-sensitive surface (emulsion) responds in a particular way to the combination of light rays which form a particular image. As we cannot see well in dim light, film emulsion cannot respond adequately to light below certain levels of intensity. Conversely, too much light can overwhelm the emulsion and result in a washed out image on the film. The emulsion speed of a given film, like eye sensitivity, is essentially a constant, with lens settings as related variables. Much as eye muscles must change the settings of the pupil and the lens to transmit light to the retina in acceptable form, the aperture and focus of a camera lens must be adjusted to fit the light from a scene to the demands of the film.

FILM AND COLOR PROBLEMS

Newsfilm reporting, by the simplest definition, consists of putting the images and sounds of news on a narrow strip of material called motion picture film.

Film Structure

The films most used in television are *16mm* wide and are fed through the camera from one reel to another. Most silent cameras are made for 100-foot reels, and a larger one can be run through only by attaching a separate magazine to hold the film. Sound cameras are

54

most often fed from 200- or 400-foot magazines, though larger ones are available.

Single-perforated film has sprocket holes along only one edge and is more commonly used than *double-perforated* film, which has sprocket holes along both edges. Sound film is single-perforated, because the sound track uses part of the surface where the holes go on double-perforated film. One use of double-perf film is to reverse action, as in making a swimmer appear to "un-dive" from the water back up to the diving board. For this effect, shoot the normal dive with double-perf film in a camera held upside down. When the film has been processed, switch head and tail of the shot and the action will be reversed. Such turning around of single-perf film would not work, because the perfs would be on the wrong side for the single row of sprockets on the feed wheels of a normal projector.

The underside of raw film as it comes off the reel is coated with the *emulsion* layers which record the image. The other side is the *base*, which is the main body of the film. Most films used in television news have a base made of a cellulose ester called triacetate. Emulsion is sensitive not only to light but to finger smudges, abrasion from rubbing against a camera body and even from the static electricity which can result from careless handling of film in a darkroom. Any touching of film surface should be against the base rather than emulsion side. The base is the glossier of the two sides.

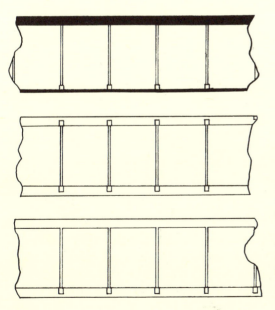

THE 16mm FILMS most used in television news are single-perforated silent (left), double-perforated silent (center), and magnetic sound-on-film (right). A stripe of magnetic coating provides the sound track for the SOF, and the narrow stripe between the perforations and the other edge is balance stripe.

Magnetic sound tracks have become standard for recording sound on film for TV news. The track consists of a layer of brown *magnetic stripe* which has been applied on the base side of the film along the edge which is not perforated. The stripe looks like a narrow audio tape, which is essentially what it is. A narrower band of *"balance stripe"* is located on the perforated side to keep the film rolling straight on its core.

TV uses color film almost exclusively. No consideration will be given the relatively simple use of black-and-white film.

The color films most used in television news when this book was written were KODAK EKTACHROME *EF Films 7241* (Daylight) and *7242 (Tungsten)*. Both are *reversal* films. Though the image is originally recorded on the film negatively, a reversal process takes place in the processing machine so that the film comes out with a positive image.

Films and Filters

Film's greatest failing in comparison to the human eye is its relatively low ability to interpret color accurately under varying light conditions. The eye and brain follow colors fairly truly from daylight to tungsten to fluorescent lights, but color film moving from one of these light sources to another can give unreal effects if the right corrective filter is not used.

An *80A filter* is normally used with EF Daylight film to correct color for the film's use under tungsten light.

An *85B filter* is the one most often used with EF Tungsten film to correct for daylight color. Unfiltered, this film is intended only for tungsten or photo lights.

The *emulsion speed* indicates how *fast* (sensitive to light intensity) the film is. EF Daylight has an exposure index of a fast ASA 160 unfiltered and a rather *slow* ASA 40 when the 80A filter is added for indoor use. EF Tungsten is rated at a fast ASA 125 under tungsten or photo lights and a moderately fast ASA 80 when the 85B filter is added for daylight shooting.

The high speed of EF 7241 often makes a *neutral density filter* necessary. The minimum opening of f/16 or f/22 on most lenses may still let in too much light on a sunny day. An ND filter reduces light intensity without affecting colors. These filters are available in densities ranging from very light (0.1ND for increasing the effective f by ⅓ stop) to very heavy filtration (4.0ND for adding 13⅓ f/stops). Choose the one best suited to your needs. The 0.3ND and 0.6 ND, which reduce exposure by 1 and 2 f/stops respectively, are much used.

EF 7242 rated at ASA 80 with an 85B filter may also be too fast in bright sunlight if the lens stops down only to f/16, as is the case for many commonly used wide angle lenses. A solution is a combination filter such as the *85BN3*, which combines 85 color correction with neutral density 0.3ND for an exposure index of ASA 40.

A filter is usually added by inserting a thin *filter holder* containing a sheet of gelatin filter material into a slot at the front of the camera. The much used Bell & Howell 70 cameras are not manufactured with filter slots but are usually so modified after purchase. The alternative of taking glass filters on and off the sleeves of individual lenses is too time-consuming to be recommended. Bolex and Scoopic cameras come with filter slots or comparable elements for easy use.

Color Temperature

Color filters are necessary because a given film is balanced for only one *color temperature,* which is expressed in degrees Kelvin and essentially indicates the extent to which light is cool (bluish) like daylight or warm (reddish) like tungsten. For example, EF 7242 Tungsten film is balanced for a color temperature of 3200°K. If this indoor-type film is shot in daylight (about 5500°K) without corrective filtering, it will have a blue cast. If it is shot unfiltered under most fluorescent lights, a green cast will result. If EF 7241 Daylight film is shot with tungsten light and without a corrective filter, it will be reddish.

Only a little wrong light can upset color balance. The governor holding a news conference in a room with several windows, even with photo lights in use, is likely to appear on film to be suffering oxygen deprivation, because of the faint bluish tinge from the sunlight in the room. Daylight can be overpowered by photo lights, but this usually requires more than you are likely to carry on a normal assignment. When in doubt with mixed light, many photographers filter as for daylight. A faint orange tinge will make the governor look suntanned rather than sick.

Fluorescent lights give more than their share of color temperature problems. Special filters such as the SR by Otivision and the FLB by Tiffen are available to correct EF 7242 film for fluorescent lighting. Tiffen also makes an FL-D filter for use with daylight film. But these filters are more effective for some types of fluorescent bulbs than for others.

One problem is that there are many types of fluorescents.

The ideal solution is for your news sources to install replacement fluorescent bulbs which have a color temperature of roughly 3200K. Then EF 7242 can be shot unfiltered with good results. Through urging from TV news organizations, some governmental agencies in Milwaukee have installed such bulbs. The same should work in other cities.

Indoor or Outdoor Film

Try to stick to the same film throughout a single story. Cutting back and forth between 7241 and 7242, for example, can call attention to color differences in the two films. Using a single type of film, with filters added as needed, also cuts down on unloading-reloading effort and the waste resulting from shooting only partial rolls of film.

Most stations have standardized on high speed indoor-type film, usually EF 7242. It combines the advantages of a relatively high film speed for use with indoor existing or photo light and easy corrective filtering for sunlight.

However, some stations have found daylight film more adaptable for general newsfilm use. Fred Brooks, news director of WBRZ-TV, Baton Rouge, La., says of EF 7241 in a staff memo:

> Although its high speed rating (ASA 160) is a bit unhandy on bright days, the film seems to have a latitude that produces acceptable color tones under most circumstances.
>
> Daylight: Good color, but a neutral density filter is necessary unless the lenses being used will close to f/22.
>
> Cloud: EF Daylight has a tendency to slightly "wash-out" color tones, resulting in a "hazy overcast" picture if the exposure is not exactly correct.
>
> Indoors: Ordinary tungsten lighting will be too red unless a proper correction filter is used. However, it is the most often acceptable of color films as an "emergency" when proper lighting is not available. Most modern offices have fluorescent lights which cause a bluish tint on tungsten film and a greenish tint on daylight film. But EF Daylight seems to give the best results when a TV portable light is used. The Sylvania Sungun seems to add just enough red to overpower the effect of the fluorescent lighting.
>
> . . . In shooting color film, think in color tones. Daylight, except around sundown, is cold (or blue). Tungsten is warm (or red) . . . EF Tungsten film turns almost completely blue if used unfiltered in daylight.

To summarize: Incandescent and photo lights are warm, and daylight and most fluorescent lights are cool in color temperature. EF Tungsten (7242) film is made for incandescent and photo lights, and is corrected for daylight and partially for fluorescent by using a No. 85B filter. EF Daylight (7241) film is made for daylight and is pretty close to correct for some fluorescent, but must be corrected for incandescent or photo lights by using a No. 80A filter.

"Pushing" Film

When film has been underexposed, some correction can be made in its processing by "pushing" (force-developing) it to a higher film speed. In pushing, the lab technician adjusts the processing machine to leave the film in the crucial first-developing tank longer, giving the chemicals more time to work at bringing out such image as may be there. The developing temperature may also be raised. Essentially, then, pushing is overdeveloping to compensate for underexposure.

Pushing should be used sparingly. It usually exacts a price in quality. Most reversal color films can be pushed the equivalent of 1 f/stop with little loss of quality and 2 stops in a bind, though this tends to give excessive contrast. Pushing more than 2 stops heightens contrast to technically undesirable extremes.

If film is to be pushed, shoot the whole roll with the same under-exposure. For example, if indoor shots are underexposed by 1 f/stop, deliberately underexpose daylight shots later in the roll by 1 stop. If you don't, the daylight shots will be washed out when force-developed along with the rest of the roll. It is asking too much of a lab technician to expect only part of a roll to be pushed.

If film requires pushing, be sure to inform the lab technician of how many f/stops the film has been underexposed.

Care of Film

Raw film that is to be stored for more than a few weeks before it is used should be kept refrigerated. The lower the *temperature*, the slower the aging which tends to deteriorate color quality. Kodak recommends a temperature of 55° F or below for periods of about 6 months.

Humidity is no problem as long as film is kept in its original taped can with the seal unbroken. When taken out of refrigeration, film should be given at least an hour and a half to warm up at room temperature before the seal is broken. Damage from moisture condensation can result from not leaving sufficient warm-up time before the seal is removed. Similarly, a little "cold-soaking" (letting film in a camera gradually drop some from room temperature) is sometimes recommended for shooting in severe cold.

When bringing exposed film in from shooting in severe cold, let it warm up a bit before loading it into a magazine for processing. Extremely cold film gets so brittle it will break easily. And when wound onto a magazine core for processing, it can generate enough static electricity to put light flashes on the film.

Even under refrigeration, film slowly deteriorates. So always rotate film stock, using the oldest film first. The regular replenishment of stocks is recommended rather than storing up very large quantities of film.

After the seal on the can has been broken, film becomes very susceptible to damage from high temperature or humidity. It should be exposed and processed as soon as possible after the package is opened. If film must be kept in a camera or magazine for more than a very few hours, try to keep it in an air-conditioned room, at least. Keep in mind, also, that exposed film deteriorates more rapidly than unexposed film.

LIGHTING

Ideally, all film would be shot with *available* light, the bulbs and windows providing the light when television is not there. The introduction of photo lights tends to change the appearance or even, by distraction, the character of an event. But sometimes there is not enough existing light for usable film. At other times photo lights may improve the technical quality of the film enough to recommend their use. *Photo lights* are either *portable* (battery operated) or the kind which are *set up* and plugged into an electrical outlet.

Available Light

The survey conducted for this book and reported in Chapter 11 indicated a trend toward increased use of available light indoors. Only a third of the newsfilm operations were making much use of indoor available light, but two of every five said they expected to do more of this in the future. Several expressed a need for faster film for such shooting.

An argument for shooting with only available light when you can is that the image tends to be truer to reality. Setup lights may make the subject look better than if television had not been there. In addition to brightening a scene, TV lights can make colors come through with fidelity unmatched in untelevised real life. Tungsten light actually is a little on the orange side, as is daylight at sundown. Fluorescent light often carries a bluish tinge for the human eye as well as for unfiltered film. On the other hand, it may be argued that true color rather than the natural scene should be the objective.

When shooting with available light, get the most out of what's there. In an office, for example, you may check to see if all lights are turned on. And sometimes taking the shade off a lamp can make the difference between a good picture and a bad one. If working off daylight indoors, you may ask to open window shades.

Available lighting may not be compatible with the automatic gain control on the film chain. If the background is extremely bright, you need to put light on the main subject. Otherwise, in transmission, the

BUILDING ON EXPERIENCE in shooting with available light, Mike Grass and other WOTV, Grand Rapids, photographers post film clips showing the results of various combinations of lighting, filters, film types and f/stops in buildings where filming is often done. The next time, the photographer filming in a particular building knows what to expect. A chart on the photo cabinet also lists results.

whole picture will be shaded down automatically, making the subject too dark, sometimes beyond recognition. Obviously you should avoid shooting into light sources, especially windows, if at all possible.

In shooting with available light, keep in mind that a wider aperture (lower f/stop) makes focus more critical. With less depth of field, be especially careful with distance settings.

Since available indoor lighting tends to be flat and dull, best results are often obtained by opening the aperture a little more than the exposure meter says, usually about half an f/stop.

Tom O'Rourke, chief photographer at WOTV, Grand Rapids, Mich., has these tips for shooting with available light indoors:

Many of the new buildings in Grand Rapids have all fluorescent lighting. We find that using Kodak 7241 with ASA 160 produces very nice color in most of the places. We also find that in the newer gyms with the mercury vapor lights, the 7241 with a 10M or 20M filter gives us the most acceptable color possible.

On our photo cabinet is a chart listing the place, type of lighting, f/stops, type of film and the results of the film as to color and exposure. When going to a new gym or other building where using TV lights is impractical, we make an educated guess as to what type of film to use and what, if any, filters to use. We then run off 10 feet of test footage—for example, 7241 with a 10M, a 20M, and no filter at all—and then shoot what we think will give the best color and exposure. When we get the film back, we compare the test footage and arrive at a decision as to what is best, or try something else. These, along with the test clips, are labeled and notations are made on our reference chart for use the next time anybody has to shoot at that location.

Portable Lights

For spot news coverage with portable lights, WOTV reported good results with a Colortran Mini Pro light, with beam booster, which O'Rourke said "really throws the light." It is mounted on a stud at the front of a sound-on-film camera and fed from a 30-volt battery pack or belt which will go 20-25 minutes on a charge. O'Rourke described the light as "ideal for fast shooting, and in certain situations all you have to do is change the cord to 120V and the bulb to a 650 watt and you have extra power and distance."

The battery-powered lights most used by stations responding to the 1973 survey conducted for this book were Frezzolini, Sylvania (usually the SG-77 or Sungun) and Colortran.

In some situations, you may get better results by holding the portable light out to the side rather than anchoring it to the camera. Although it introduces a potential for shakiness, holding the light to one side and slightly above the camera can add depth. This so-called "45 degree light" gives about the most dimension possible with a single artificial light source.

Aside from keeping the picture from being so flat, the free light approach tends to draw attention away from the camera itself, reducing the "stare into the lens" effect. It also allows you to "feather" the light, bringing it down gradually to hit the subject and reducing the "squint and flinch" reaction of a person suddenly hit by bright light.

Take advantage of any spot-to-floor adjustment on the reflector head. In most cases, the even illumination of the flood is preferable to the spot setting. At flood position, all or nearly all of the area covered by a wide angle lens will be lighted. The spot position, on the other hand, may give the impression of a flashlight in a coal mine. Reserve the spot setting for those adverse situations in which it is the only way of lighting up a limited area at a distance, for example, singling out an individual in a crowd or spotlighting a demonstrator's placard.

With some wide angle lenses, there is still some light drop-off around the edges of the frame even with the flood setting. If you can find someone to hold the light, the flashlight effect can be eliminated by having the light held just a little behind your shooting location.

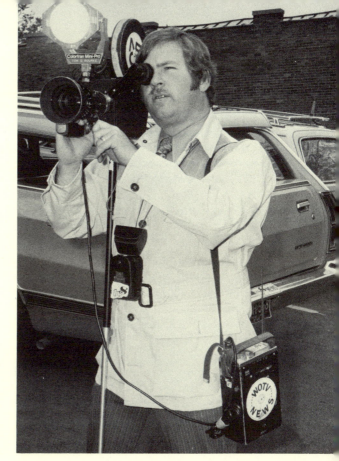

PORTABLE LIGHTING is essential for photographers like Tom O'Rourke, WOTV, Grand Rapids, for shooting natural sound-on-film. The Mini-Pro light with beam booster runs 20-25 minutes on a charge of the 30V battery pack.

Setup Lighting

In a controlled situation, such as an interview or a feature, a dull, flat-lighted picture is not necessary. A key light, fill light and back light can be set up for ample illumination. These lights are normally mounted on lightweight stands and plugged into AC electrical outlets. Modern high-intensity lights of this kind are not cumbersome. The entire setup can be packed into a large attache case.

Colortrans were the most used setup lights by three-fourths of the respondents in our 1973 survey. Most of the others were using Frezzolini, Sylvania or Smith-Victor models.

The *key light* is the principal light source, establishing the exposure setting. It is usually projected at an angle of 30–40 degrees. Putting the key light high enough that it faces down on the subject lessens squinting and shadow problems. This also reduces the problem of light glare from a subject's eyeglasses.

The *fill light*, as the name implies, fills in harsh shadows and reduces contrast for better television reproduction. A soft or diffuse light is desirable. The projection angle should be as low as practical, preferably 30 degrees or less.

The ratio of light intensity of the key to the fill is usually 2:1 to 3:1. A 2:1 ratio means the key light is one f/stop brighter on the subject than is the fill. A 3:1 ratio indicates 1½ stops difference. The higher ratio gives more molding and depth. A lower ratio flattens and is sometimes considered more realistic.

The *back light* tends to make the subject stand out from the background (no more blending into the woodwork) and adds dimension. The projection angle should not exceed 45 degrees but should be steep enough to prevent direct rays of light from falling on the camera lens. If light shines on the lens, the result will be a "flare" effect on the film. If, as sometimes happens in a small room, back lighting cannot be done without flare, the light can be turned around to light the wall behind the subject, thus becoming a "set light." While not as effective as regular back lighting, this will still separate the subject somewhat from the background and wash out shadows created by key and fill lights.

One of the most commonly used setups is "short lighting," in which the key light illuminates the side of the face turned away from the camera. "Broad lighting," by contrast, turns the key light on the side of the face toward the camera. Short lighting produces the greater modeling effect, giving an illusion of depth to the two-dimensional film.

EXPOSURE

Professionals use an *exposure meter*, a device which measures the amount of light available for filming. Only over-confident amateurs fully trust their eyes. The human eye, with its marvelous adjustment features, is not as dependable at judging light intensity as is a properly adjusted meter. At the same time, you must gain a sense of light to enable adjusting for deceptive meter readings.

The two basic types of meter readings are 1) reflected and 2) incident.

Reflected readings measure the light bouncing off the subject to be photographed. To get a reflected reading, the meter is placed between the camera and the subject, pointing toward the subject.

Incident readings measure the amount of light falling upon (rather than reflected off) the subject. For an incident reading, a translucent shield normally is moved over the meter's "eye" element, and the meter is again placed between the camera and the subject, but this time it must be pointed toward the camera. Outdoors, it is not necessary to walk to the subject if the reading can be taken in the same light

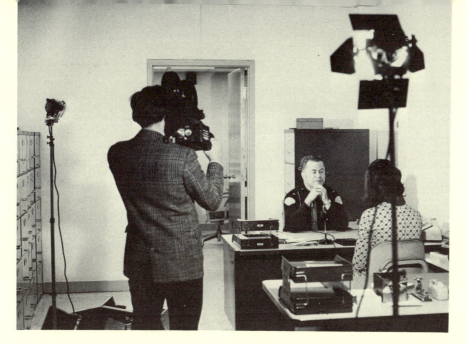

SETUP LIGHTING is used for a WBAY-TV, Green Bay, Wis., interview conducted by Sue Peterson and filmed by Steve Ellingboe. In this "broad lighting" setup, a spot on the left serves as the key light and the more diffuse "barn-doored" light on the right provides fill.

(shade, overcast, bright sunlight, etc.). But if working under artificial lights, especially in close quarters, you must take the reading right at the subject to be accurate. Readings closer to artificial lights will be too high and the film too dark.

In general, reflected readings are preferred because they take into account the flesh tones of the subject and brightness contrast within the scene. You may wish, however, to take an incident reading as a double check on the accuracy of your reflected reading. If the readings are grossly discrepant, at least one reading is incorrect.

The only setting required on most meters is for the ASA (emulsion speed) of the film.

In taking a reflected light reading, be sure the light measured is from the subject, not directly from a light source. Especially in using available light indoors, avoid taking readings too close to light sources such as windows or lamps. The result can be falsely high readings and underexposure of the film. Your hand can be used to shield the meter from strong light coming in from the sides or above which might give a deceptive reading. But be careful not to block out any of the light from the subject with your hand.

A false reading can come from casting a shadow on the subject. Also, observe the manufacturer's recommended way of holding the meter. It is possible to tilt some meters until, by the needle's own weight, it will fall into a false reading.

THE EXPOSURE METER READ-
ING for the filming shown on this
book's cover was taken with a
Gossen Luna Pro. Note also how
Tom O'Rourke of WOTV, Grand
Rapids, uses a monopod to add
support to the shoulder-balanced
camera.

The best general rule is to take the reading at the center of interest for the particular scene. If interested in the full wide scene, then a reading off the wide scene is what you want. However, if the center of attraction is a face, then get the reading off the face and don't worry if the background is somewhat brighter. If you expose for the brighter background, the face will be dark.

Faces usually are enhanced by exposing just slightly more than the meter says—a half stop or so in most cases.

It is not necessary to stick the meter in the news source's face. A reflected light reading off the palm of your hand, properly held, can give a reasonably accurate approximation of what the light is like on the subject's face.

Exposure meter readings must sometimes be tempered with your judgment, especially in high-contrast light situations. Indeed, you should avoid extreme contrast within shots as much as possible. Projection equipment at many stations automatically balances the image in such a way as to darken the face which you properly exposed against a sunny sky which you intended to let wash out as background. High contrast is part of reality, but one which the electronic equipment of television will not fully accept.

What if your experience tells you the reading just could not be right? For example, you are getting f/8 in bright sun or f/11 with natural light in an office? Don't just go ahead and mechanically shoot at a setting you are convinced is far off. Instead, check to see what's wrong—with the meter or the way you are using it.

Bad exposure will more likely be your fault than the meter's, because the ones most used in TV are pretty reliable. Gossen, Sekonic and Spectra meters were the ones most used by respondents in our 1973 newsfilm survey, and high user satisfaction was indicated for all three brands.

It is not always possible to take a meter reading at the scene of a news event. As soon as possible, you should develop a feeling for various lighting situations and the ability to approximate the proper f/stops. Then, if unable to take a reading, you should still be close enough for usable film. In no other area of newsfilm is the ability to learn from experience more important.

REMINDERS

- EF 7241 film is used unfiltered in daylight and with an 80A filter for tungsten or movie lights.
- EF 7242 is used unfiltered for tungsten or movie lights and with an 85B filter for daylight.
- Fluorescent bulbs vary in color temperature, but most are better treated as daylight than as tungsten. Special filters can help.
- Keep film in a cool place as much as possible.
- When shooting with available light indoors, it often helps to open up half an f/stop wider than the meter indicates.
- Avoid shooting into light sources, particularly windows.
- The flood usually gives more pleasing results than the spot setting on portable lights.
- A key light is often supplemented with a fill light to reduce shadows and contrast and a back light to add dimension.
- Reflected readings on an exposure meter measure the light bouncing off the subject, and incident readings measure the light falling upon the subject.
- In taking meter readings, avoid getting too close to artificial lights or casting a shadow on the subject.
- Meter readings must sometimes be tempered by your judgment.

5 | The Sound of Reality

When Willie Mays retired from baseball in 1973, a network ran film flashbacks from his career. Something seemed strangely missing. What was it? Sound. We saw but did not hear the pops of the bat, the cheers of the crowds. On a network where natural sound had become the rule for sports film, the silence of the old Mays action footage seemed almost eerie. Indeed, it was more so than when originally shown, because in the earlier years of television, background music was usually played behind action film. Even silent movies of the 1920s were accompanied by live player piano or organ music. From the beginning, people working with film have been aware that total silence is a conspicuous violation of most reality.

Television news is increasingly treating sound as an integral part of most stories. When surveyed for this book, newsfilm operations represented by RTNDA members overwhelmingly reported that they were moving toward the use of natural sound in place of silent film. Stations which continue to show much silent film of meetings, audiences, parades or school rooms, for example, will tend to look as out of date as if they were still filming in black-and-white.

SOUND-ON-FILM EQUIPMENT

If you have mastered silent shooting, moving to sound-on-film equipment should not be difficult. Most modern sound cameras are fairly easy to operate, easier than many silent cameras in some respects. For example, there is no more winding of the kind you must do with most silent cameras.

Single and Double-System

Most sound film for television news is shot with *single-system* sound, which means the picture and sound are recorded on the same (single) strip of film. The sound is recorded 28 frames ahead of the picture on a magnetic tape stripe which runs along the edge of the film. The main disadvantage of single-system sound is in editing film with a gap of just over 1 second between sound and picture. Its main advantage is that single-system equipment is portable, compact and relatively easy and economical to operate.

Double-system equipment records the sound, not on the film with the picture, but on a separate tape or sprocketed magnetic film. A special tape recorder, such as models made by Nagra, is usually used for sound pickup. The separate audio and film systems must be synchronized, of course. A *sync-signal* which will later keep audio and image precisely together is put on the magnetic tape without interfering with the sound. With a battery-operated, quartz-crystal-controlled camera and recorder motor, this can be done without a cable linking the camera with the audio system. The main disadvantages of double-system have been its cumbersomeness, time-consuming sound transfers, slower editing with most older equipment, and the necessity for more expensive editing and projection equipment if news deadlines are to be met. Its main advantage is in the cleaner editing which it permits.

Improved equipment is making double-system somewhat more attractive for news. The RTNDA newsfilm survey reported in Chapter 11 indicated a moderate trend toward its increased use. Though very few operations were using much double-system in 1973, one-fifth said the trend at their stations was toward increased use.

Sound Cameras

For years the standard cameras for shooting single-system sound for television news were Auricons. But even with conversions to make them more portable, they remained heavier and less compact than desirable. Combat photography in the Vietnam War in the 1960s brought demands for greater camera mobility, and improved units began to appear. By the early 1970s, new sound cameras designed expressly for the needs of TV news were readily available and were the ones most often being purchased.

The most popular SOF cameras as this was being written included the CP-16/A by Cinema Products, the Frezzi-Cordless LW-16 and the Canon Sound Scoopic. All are lightweight, truly portable cameras designed for the *"one-man band"* operation whereby a single person shoots the film, controls the sound and handles any special lighting for TV.

Modern cameras have built-in or attached amplifiers and batteries as part of a single shoulder-balanced unit weighing 15-17 pounds when equipped with a 400-foot *magazine* fully loaded with enough film for just under 11 minutes of shooting. For longer jobs, additional pre-loaded 400-foot magazines may be taken along, or magazines holding 600, 800 or 1,200 feet may be used.

The newer TV-designed cameras do away with most of the cords which impede maneuverability with older models. Rather than being separate units linked to the camera by cords, a lightweight *battery* and *amplifier* are now built in or attached to the camera body so as to make a single unit. If operating off the battery and using a microphone attached to the top of the camera, sound-on-film can be shot with the mobility of silent film.

Accessories

A sound camera is normally equipped with a zoom lens, such as an Angenieux 12-120mm or the 9.5-57mm for wider angle and larger aperture (f/1.6) for low light levels. Shoulder-braced cameras need viewfinders which will extend out to the side rather than only toward the back of the camera.

High quality *microphones* are a good investment. The thousands of dollars paid for a sound camera are partially wasted if the sound is fed into it from an inadequate mike. Camera manufacturers and station engineers are often good sources as to the best microphones for a particular camera and various shooting situations. Many kinds of hand microphones are available. Some stations also use shotgun mikes. These long, highly directional microphones can reach out and isolate sound some distance away. The camera reporter, especially when working alone, becomes more mobile by attaching a shotgun mike to the sound camera. Another attraction is that this mike seldom need show in the picture. But shotgun mikes require careful use. Background noises can easily come through too strongly, and turning the mike slightly off direction can cause you to practically lose the voice of a speaker.

The noise of wind blowing against a microphone can be reduced by covering it with a *windscreen,* a device usually made of foam material. (Windscreens are shown in photos on pages 95 and 97.) A screen can be improvised from packing foam, a soft sock or other cloth. And, of

THE CINEMA PRODUCTS CP-16/A sound-on-film camera puts everything, including amplifier and battery, into a single shoulder-balanced unit. A shoulder pod often used with the camera is not shown. The Mitchell magazine holds 400 feet of film, and the lens is an Angenieux 12-120mm zoom. The microphone is an RE50 and the light a CP Sturdy-Lite quartz focusing spot (600 watt, 120 volt AC/DC or 250 watt, 30 volt battery operation).

THE FREZZI-CORDLESS LW-16 camera has amplifier and battery attached as part of the shoulder-podded unit. It is shown geared for two-microphone operation. A light can be mounted atop the camera. The Mitchell magazine holds 400 feet of film, and the lens is an Angenieux 12-120mm zoom.

course, you can use your body and other natural shields to help keep wind off the microphone surface.

Cameras such as the CP-16/A and Frezzi-Cordless LW-16 are designed to rest on the shoulder, with comfort enhanced by adding a lightweight *shoulder pod,* which puts padding between camera and shoulder. A *body brace,* often used with older cameras, tends to put more strain on the back.

A *tripod* gives the sturdiest camera support and is especially recommended when shakiness may be a problem, as in using a telephoto lens on a speaker. Some photographers find that a *monopod* (shown in photos on pages 63 and 66) is adequate for many situations.

Photo lights and *exposure meters* are discussed in Chapter 4.

The Package

The combination of equipment should be coordinated to fit the coverage needs of your particular station. Camera manufacturers often serve as consultants for station or network needs, custom-designing a camera and its accessories to its purchaser's requirements. An important factor is whether you normally work as part of a crew of two or three or operate as a "one-man band." With the coming of truly portable equipment, one person is doing the whole job of newsfilming with sound at many stations.

Basic equipment used for the "one-man band" work at medium market WOTV, Grand Rapids, is described by chief photographer Tom O'Rourke:

> The trend here is toward more mobility and sound on every piece of film shot—sound-on-film or sound-under. We are a one-man band doing shooting, lighting and running audio level. The CP-16/A makes a nice 16-pound package with automatic gain controls.
>
> Steadiness is not a problem because our talking heads are usually shot at 6-7 feet distance with a monopod being used when possible.
>
> The CP-16/A and the Mini Pro lights have the flexibility and durability to make shooting very fast and effective. And the fact that you don't have cables and light stands all over the place makes most meetings and interviews more relaxed.
>
> A tool we have found most effective is the AKG condenser shotgun mike that reaches out and literally isolates an individual or group. Even 15-20 feet away, it produces acceptable sound, and with no mike sticking up close in a subject's face, more spontaneity, is evident. At meetings our reporter often holds the mike. With a little practice, a photographer can do it himself.
>
> Again, our goal is to give the maximum amount of coverage with the least amount of disruptions. By using the type of equipment available today, there is no need for photo crews to disrupt proceedings with light stands, cables and bulky tripods.

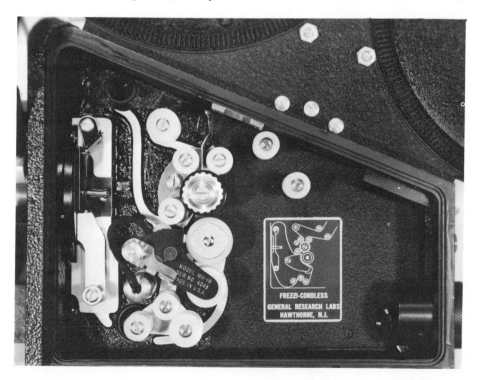

THE CANON SOUND SCOOPIC is a compact body-braced camera which can be powered by a light-weight battery enclosed in the amplifier case, which can be hung from a shoulder strap. The lens is a Canon 12.5-75mm zoom. Automatic exposure control can be overridden.

THREADING A SOUND CAMERA is easy if you follow the **threading diagram** included on the inside of most cameras. Most Auricons, **Frezzis and CPs are threaded in** essentially the same way.

A BODY BRACE puts the weight out front, and some photographers and find it tiring on the back. Carroll Darringer shoots sound-on-film as a "one-man crew" at WMT-TV, Cedar Rapids, Iowa. The camera is a Frezzolini conversion of an Auricon Cine-Voice.

SHOULDER-BALANCED cameras minimize back strain. An LW-16 is demonstrated by James J. Crawford, vice-president for engineering, Frezzolini Electronics, Inc. Note the differences in size and ease of handling between this camera and the older Frezzi shown above.

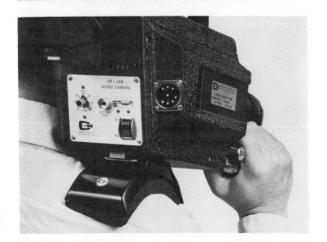

A SHOULDER POD gives comfortable support for shoulder-balanced cameras such as the CP-16 models and the Frezzi-Cordless LW-16.

Camera Operation

Modern sound cameras are fairly easy to operate, and the best guides to the mechanical aspects are the instruction manuals for particular cameras. However, a few general principles apply to most cameras.

The distance from the film gate aperture (where the picture is taken) to the pickup head (where the sound is recorded) on single-system film must be exactly 28 *frames*. Being off even a couple of frames can cause a noticeable lack of lip synch.

Always let the camera run for a few seconds before the sound you want begins and at least 2 or 3 seconds beyond the finish of a take. Otherwise, editing problems can result.

In shooting SOF, you must be aware of what is going on the sound track as well as the image going on the film emulsion. Unless using automatic gain control, be particularly alert for the changing loudness of sound entering the amplifier. Speakers move, their volume or inflection changes, room noise grows or lessens, all affecting the sound level being recorded. This level is indicated by a VU meter on the amplifier, and regulating the sound level is called "riding gain."

As assurance against getting unusable sound, *monitor* the sound (listen through an earphone) from "playback" rather than "record" if your camera permits. "Playback" lets you hear the sound which has already been recorded on the film's magnetic stripe a split second earlier. Use the "record" or "microphone" position of the switch only to set a level and check out the system prior to shooting. While shooting, keep the switch on "playback" or "film monitor" to afford a continuous check of what is on the sound track.

The automatic gain control (AGC) found on many cameras can usually control effectively for ups and downs of sound level in speeches, office interviews and other situations with minimal background noise. But on many occasions, especially in noisy outdoor settings, veterans like Joe Sullivan, newsfilm manager at WCCO-TV, Minneapolis, will keep the AGC off and control the voice level themselves. Says Sullivan: "At a fire, for instance, where there are a lot of pumpers and other equipment making background noise, an interview with the fire chief is very disturbed by the AGC's 'seeking,' that is, bringing up the volume of background sound during pauses in the interview."

Sound-on-film may be divided generally into two categories: 1) *voice* or "talking head" sound, an interview or the like, in which talking is the main element; and 2) *natural* sound, as of demonstrators chanting or an audience sitting in what may seem silence but which is never total silence.

VOICE SOUND

Voice sound is often called setup sound, because the sound gear and lights may usually be "set up" carefully in advance of the event—which in most cases is a speech, news conference or interview. These are television's "talking heads," a term which has developed from the tendency by lazy, unimaginative news operations to show officials and others merely talking about situations rather than showing film of the situations themselves.

Microphone placement is usually a matter of compromise. Ideally, the viewer should not be conscious of the microphone, but this is often unavoidable. The mike must be close enough to the subject to obtain an adequate sound level. In general, the lower the VU meter level at which you can ride a mike, the cleaner the sound. To use the lower pickup gain, you must usually put the mike in fairly close.

Microphones used with most equipment are best spoken across, not into. Harsh consonants spoken directly into a microphone, especially at close range, may cause an annoying "hiss" (sibilance) or "pop" on the sound track.

Avoid *background noises* which will be conspicuously nonconsecutive when the film has been edited. Music from a radio in the background will come through on edited film like a pickup arm jumping tracks on a phonograph record.

Background noises can also be so loud that they make it hard to follow what the speaker is saying. Interviewing the street superintendent while a worker bangs away with a steam hammer in the background may be naturalistic, but if we are unable to understand what is being said, the film is wasted. The voice should take priority in voice SOF. Natural background sounds are fine when appropriate, but only so long as they do not impede communication.

Visual considerations for SOF are similar to those for silent film. For example, in composition, avoid putting the talking head in the exact center of the frame. If looking to the left of the screen, the head should be slightly off center to the right. And don't lose a moving subject with too tight a shot.

Excessive *zooming* is as out of place in speech or interview SOF as elsewhere. Shots should be varied to provide visual relief in a long interview or speech. But they should normally be complete changes from shot to shot, as in going directly from 25mm to 75mm focal length, rather than zoom-ins and zoom-outs. If you must zoom while the camera is running, try to do it on the reporter's question in an interview or seemingly routine content in a speech. This makes it easier to edit out the zoom later.

VOICE SOUND-ON-FILM is used for interviews, speeches, etc. David Glodt of KTRK, Houston, interviews Mrs. Lyndon B. Johnson at the Johnson ranch near Austin. A natural setting such as this, with the low level sounds of cattle in the background, can make the interview film more interesting. But don't let the background sound interfere with the voice sound.

The standard interview which is shot with a single SOF camera can be given a two-camera effect at the editing bench if you shoot "reversals" of the reporter re-asking the questions after the interview is over. These more or less head-on shots of the reporter are later spliced in to replace those taken when the camera was facing the interviewee. But caution is in order. Reversals too often look just a bit contrived to the discerning viewer. Unless the reporter is a better actor than most, the questions re-stated when the interview is over will look and sound a little too smooth for reality, too calculated or rehearsed, too responsive to the photographer's cue—in other words, staged. Your best bet for a reversal that looks natural is to have the reporter actually re-ask the question of the interviewee. Visual continuity can be added by shooting some of the reversals to show part of the interviewee from over the shoulder.

The overuse of "talking heads" has brought criticism from such news directors as Ron Handberg, WCCO-TV, Minneapolis:

Some of the electricity has left our electronic product, and I blame much of the loss on the emergence of what I have heard described as "the talking head."

A talking head, by way of definition, is an interviewee. Plain and simple. An in-focus, well-framed head. That talks. It can be male or female, literate or illiterate, liberal or conservative, a big name or a nobody . . . Nine out of ten will put you to sleep before the first commercial.

How much better, for instance, to forget about using news conference film of a talking head describing a new housing project and
instead go out to demonstrate visually what the new project is going to
mean to the people of the neighborhood.

I am aware that many stations are doing that kind of thing now,
and have been. But many are not, and an increasing number, I think,
are taking the easy way out, falling prey to the temptation to go with
the talking head.

Handberg emphasizes that his objection is not to interviewees such
as the woman whose home has been flooded or the people seen with
Charles Kuralt in the CBS "On the Road" reports. Talking heads can be
interesting. But such is often not the case when someone reads a
statement, makes an announcement or routine speech, or is interviewed
in an office. This kind of film is usually good only for short takes unless covered visually by B-roll, to be discussed later. Always ask yourself—is voice SOF the best way to tell the story? It is usually the easiest,
but often not the best.

NATURAL SOUND

For most newsfilm, total silence is unnatural. To see but not to
hear applause, traffic, construction or grocery shopping is not to be a
witness to full reality. Sound is part of a person's "presence" anywhere.
Even in a seemingly silent room or landscape setting, a low level of
sound, more distinctive than you might think, is part of the reality.
Film without sound usually lacks a dimension which is part of the
real world.

For example, the old practice of shooting silent establishing and
cutaway shots to be edited around sound film may give unrealistic results. Going from full sound to sudden silence amounts to an audio
jump cut that jolts the ear as surely as putting together two almost but
not quite identical scenes jolts the eye. Networks and many local
stations shoot most establishing shots, audience cutaways, etc., with
sound cameras.

But natural sound does not come naturally just because you are
using an SOF camera.

Natural sound is usually an adjunct to the visual message and
should be considered in terms of whether it adds or detracts from the
story.

Limitations of equipment enter into this consideration. For example, gunfire and explosions seldom sound "natural" on a single-system sound track. Microphones used with most sound cameras are

not as discriminating as the human ear in the sense of being able to concentrate on a single characteristic sound. What is recorded on the sound stripe is a mixture of all the audible inputs. Distinctive sounds can thus become "homogenized" into a single "whoosh" that sounds more like faulty equipment than "presence."

Microphone placement is critical in the proper recording of natural sound, just as it is with voice sound. A single microphone tends to pick up sounds closest to it out of all proportion to the average sound level in an area as heard by the human ear. For this reason, it is sometimes recommended that the microphone be farther back than the camera for wide shots. Microphones can also pick up camera noise. And if the amplifier must "strain" by running at excessively high gain to record the "natural" sound, the result is anything but natural. It is more likely to be mushy and indistinguishable—that omnipresent "whoosh."

While shooting excess natural sound on film is to be discouraged, so is shooting for too short a time. Natural sound shots should be allowed to *run longer* than silent shots of an event, or there may be too many noticeable jumps in audio.

NATURAL SOUND-ON-FILM of a meeting adds a dimension missing in silent film. Claudia Danovic and others at WDAY-TV, Fargo, N.D., shoot natural sound with practically all stories when using the Canon Sound Scoopic and decide later whether to use the sound under the reporter's voice. A 635A microphone is taped to the power cable for picking up the natural sound.

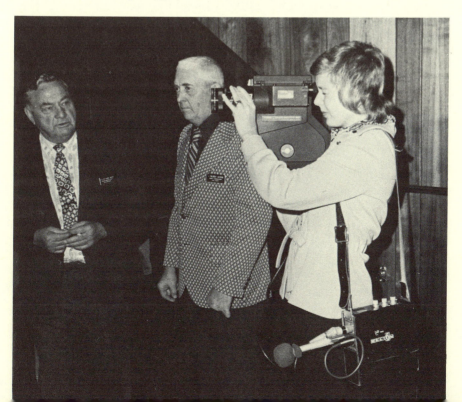

Continuity of sound is as important as continuity of picture. It is often easier for nonconsecutive shots to look consecutive than to sound that way. Audio "jump cuts" can be quite discernible. This is why natural sound shots of parades, demonstrations, traffic, etc., need to run longer than if you were shooting silent. With good natural sound, too, the sound enables a shot to sustain interest for a longer time. One reason that relatively short shots are usually recommended for silent film is that, without sound, more visual variety is needed to sustain interest.

The increased use of natural sound has re-introduced one of the basic concerns of newsfilm quality—*shakiness*. The use of a heavy shoulder-mounted rig with trailing wires, a portable power supply, etc., militates against steady pictures. Again, as in so many aspects of news-film work, it is a point of compromise. If the value of the sound track outweighs a little camera movement, fine. If not, perhaps steadier film should take priority over the natural sound. If a technique does not enhance communication, it is best not used.

WILD SOUND

In situations where shooting SOF is impractical, a cassette audio tape recorder can be used to pick up the natural sounds of the event. When this physically separate ("wild") audio is played while the film is being shown, the result is called "wild sound."

Wild sound back of film can be quite effective in some situations. The taped sounds of rush hour traffic, earth-moving equipment at work, or a blizzard's winds are among those that tend to go easily with appropriate film.

You can also put short recorded excerpts of a person talking behind film illustrating the topic. For example, the recorded words of a state official may be brought in behind film of flood damage. In most cases, "Voice of _____" should be superimposed at the bottom of the screen at this point.

Do not run wild sound of a voice while film is showing lip movement for the same words. You won't get lip synchronization. What the viewer sees and hears the speaker saying will annoyingly be not quite the same.

REMINDERS

- Sound is recorded on a magnetic stripe along the edge of the film in single-system and on a separate magnetic reel in double-system.
- Single-system sound is recorded 28 frames ahead of the picture.
- Run the SOF camera a few seconds before and after the desired shot to minimize editing problems.
- "Riding gain" is monitoring sound and adjusting the level as needed. Monitoring should be from "playback" rather than "record" if the camera permits.
- Voice SOF is of people talking (interviews, speeches, etc.) and natural SOF is the sound of scenes (crowds, traffic, etc.).
- Avoid excessive zooming.
- When zooming on an interview, normally do it on the reporter's question.
- Shoot reversals while the interviewee is still present.
- Monitor the sound carefully in shooting natural SOF to counter tendencies for such sounds to homogenize into a "whoosh" and for those closest to the microphone to be over-emphasized.
- Allow natural SOF shots to run longer than silent shots, to minimize noticeable jumps in audio.
- Silent film can often be enhanced by adding "wild" sound recorded separately on an audio cassette tape.

6 | Camera Reporting

Using the newsfilm camera as a tool for reporting is the object of the techniques described in the preceding chapters. Field reporting through the eye of a camera and the ear of a microphone can be one of the most exciting and challenging assignments in television. But if you have not become reasonably comfortable with the equipment *before* going out, it can be a frustrating, wasteful ordeal.

Only if you have mastered such techniques as holding the camera steady, taking light readings, setting lenses, composing shots and thinking in story-telling sequences—are you ready to go out on your first film story. Let plenty of practice on these basics come first.

Learning is cumulative. So try to keep it simple at the start. Ideally, your first story will be with a silent camera in daylight. Advance next to silent shooting in photo-light situations. Then, with some successful silent camera-reporting to your credit, take out the sound camera, first in setup situations where there is plenty of time to check things carefully, and finally shoulder-podded or body-braced for natural SOF reporting of an action story.

We repeat: Don't be overwhelmed. But don't be over-confident. The professional approach combines confidence with constant alertness.

EQUIPMENT IN THE FIELD

Know your equipment, care for it and always leave it ready for use—by you or someone else. Know what you need and check to be sure you have it before leaving for the story.

What You'll Need

At least at the start, check equipment needs against a written list. The list will vary by station, equipment and story. But yours can begin with the following:

For silent. Routinely take: camera loaded with appropriate film . . . exposure meter . . . filters . . . extra film . . . extra film can and take-up reel . . . note pad and at least two pens or pencils.

You may also need: lights and extension cords . . . tape measure . . . tripod . . . cassette tape recorder and cassette.

For sound. To shoot SOF with the equipment most in use in 1973, the list might resemble one prepared at WWBT, Richmond, Va.: sound camera with 12-120mm lens . . . two loaded 400-foot film magazines . . . sound amplifier and cables . . . microphones and stands . . . battery pack . . . tripod . . . shoulder brace . . . lights, light stands and electrical cable . . . cases for equipment.

In addition, most of the items listed for silent shooting are needed for SOF as well. But with modern equipment, the entire package can be surprisingly compact.

Carry in the car. A newsfilm photographer should use the same vehicle as much as possible and find room in it for such items as: 3-way electrical plugs . . . spare battery pack . . . empty cans and takeup reels . . . manila envelopes for sending film and notes back . . . lens cleaning tissue . . . soft lint-free cloth brush for cleaning cameras . . . spare photo-light bulbs and camera amplifier fuses . . . electrical tape (for repairs, cord-splicing, hanging lights, or taping microphones securely to small rostrums) . . . screwdriver, pliers and other hand tools as needed.

Sounds as if you're going to set up a studio? At some time or other you'll need it all, and probably some items not listed here. For example, experience and some big cleaning bills have indicated an occasional need for such things as coveralls, boots, gloves, hard hat, flashlight with extra batteries, first-aid kit and even a gas mask for some situations.

Double check. No matter how big or urgent the story, keep a cool head and spend those extra few seconds necessary to check to be sure you have everything you need to shoot it. What can happen when the "excitables" take over is described by Ed Dooks of WBZ-TV, Boston, in his presentation for the 1973 "Flying Short Course" conducted for news photographers in four major cities and sponsored by the National Press Photographers Association and the Department of Defense. As Dooks tells it:

A newsfilm photographer was sent to the scene of a jail break to get sound-on-film. He was physically pushed out the door by a news director who got quite excited when a spot news story was developing. In his haste he did not allow the man that extra few seconds to check if he had everything. He arrived at the scene with reporter and sound rig—but no battery pack to make the sound rig go.

Know where things are. This may seem obvious, but too many beginners waste time looking for things. Veterans like Dooks have learned the importance of orderliness. Dooks advises:

Standardize your work habits. In a news emergency you will respond out of habit. This will mean time saved since you won't wonder where you put this piece of equipment or if you have forgotten that piece of equipment. In my car the hand camera is on the rear seat behind the driver's seat with the Frezzi below it on the floor. The film supply is in the middle of the rear seat. How many of you carry empty reels and cans for shipping film if you need to? The sound rig is on the left of the tailgate directly in front of the box of lights, and the light stands and tripod with the two-wheel dolly to carry all that junk is on the right. I keep the daylight conversion filter out of the camera unless I need it since most of my assignments are with tungsten light. In the sound rig the mike cables and mikes are in the small compartment, AC power cords are in the open compartment, and the accessories such as batteries, spare light bulbs, small set of tools, pad, cords, etc., are in the large compartment.

Equipment Care

Take care of equipment and film.
Some general rules:
Don't leave film in hot, direct sunlight.
Check lenses often and clean them of spots of rain or snow.
Don't touch halogen photo light bulbs. The slightest finger smudge can cause the bulb to blow out.
Keep cameras clean. A collection of dust, sand or bits of emulsion inside a camera can damage the film as well as the mechanism. A bit of lint in the film gate can come through like an octopus waving from around the edge of the frame.
Sand can ruin a camera's motor.
Keep the camera as dry as possible. If it gets wet, clean and dry it right away. Water working its way into the mechanism can ruin it. Salt water is especially hazardous.
Don't leave equipment unattended except in a locked vehicle, and then conceal it as much as possible. Expensive film equipment attracts thieves.

When a piece of gear malfunctions, never leave it unmarked on the shelf. The person who picks it up unknowingly may lose a story by assuming that everything is in operating condition.

When you remove film from a camera, leaving a partial unexposed roll in the camera, be sure to attach another takeup reel to replace the one you removed. Also, if leaving a partial roll of film in a camera, tape on a note telling how much of what kind of film.

In cold weather. Film journalists in Miami and Houston may skip this section, but those in Milwaukee and Fargo should read on. Newsfilm equipment requires special care when temperatures or chill factors get down around zero.

A camera can freeze up on you. Carrying it under your coat can help, as can hitting the trigger for a frame or two occasionally. And since the cold camera spring is stiff, avoid winding it to full crank.

At WBAY-TV, Green Bay, Wis., News Director Jim Marshall says the toughest problem is to keep a camera running for three hours during a football game. His staff uses "head lamps" (similar to sun lamps) and/or electric blankets/heating pads where electricity is available and portable propane heaters where it is not. Jon-e hand warmers are sometimes attached to the side of WBAY-TV cameras.

The makers of the newer sound-on-film cameras claim efficient operation for this gear in severe cold. The Frezzolini LW16, for example, is rated as functional at temperatures as low as 10 below zero Fahrenheit.

But no camera will run for long if the battery gets too cold. Marshall suggests that you carry two batteries, keeping one between your belt and body, and alternating them. Between stories, put the body-warmed battery in the camera and the cold one under your belt.

Gordon Yoder, Dallas, veteran supplier of SOF newsfilm equipment, advises:

> The first thing I suggest for winterization of a camera is a complete cleaning and lubrication with proper lubricants. . . . Cameras should be overhauled at least once a year, preferably at the end of summer in preparation for winter problems. . . . Lubricate with the regular silicone lubricant. . . . This works on Auricon conversions, or Frezzolini, or CP-16, etc. . . . Do not mix regular oil with this under any circumstances. Oil and silicone do not mix!

What of steaming lenses? When a cold camera is brought into a warm room, condensation on lenses is almost inevitable. If possible, allow time for the condensing to stop. If the lens is wiped while still very cold, it will just steam up again.

Cold weather problems are routine in Fargo, North Dakota, where WDAY-TV News Director Norm Schrader has found the following practices to work:

> In winter our news wagon is never allowed to get cold. Parked at the station during the day or at the photographer's home at night, we hook it up to 110 volt power to operate an electric car heater. (Carter makes an 850 watt unit which fits under the dash.) . . . The interior of the vehicle isn't allowed to get cold, or the equipment therein, all winter.
>
> We never carry cameras in the front seat, always in the rear. This virtually eliminates lens steaming.
>
> After shooting in the cold and returning to the station, we leave the camera open to air dry before re-loading. Leaving moisture (from cold air shooting) locked up with a re-load will guarantee a freeze-up in sub-zero cold. . . .
>
> We charge any used battery immediately upon returning from a a story. All batteries are charged once a week whether they have been used or not. . . .
>
> When out in the cold for a period of time, the cameraman puts the Frezzi power pack under his outer coat to keep it warm. Same with the silent camera. Sometimes we pack a tripod-SOF camera in Jon-e hand warmers and blimp it with a blanket.
>
> We oil our cameras once a year, in the spring. Oiling in winter means the camera will freeze in subzero weather. We use the B&H, Bolex and Canon Scoopic. The oiling rule applies to all three.
>
> We have learned painfully that well charged batteries and the absence of fall oiling are the most important rules to follow.

Note that Yoder lubricates with silicone in the fall, but Schrader uses oil and only in the spring.

GETTING THE STORY

Though camera reporting can be learned only by experience, the process may be easier if you are aware of some things the authors and others have learned over the years, often the hard way.

Plan Ahead

Some film sequences require controlled conditions and can be obtained only with advance planning and special arrangements.

For example, if B-roll film is needed for a factory production process or hospital conditions, don't count on being able just to barge in unannounced and shoot the film. Call in advance. In many cases there will be an official of the agency or firm in charge of media relations. And in most cases you will get cooperation if you approach the situation maturely. But if you go charging in with an overbearing "Casey the great" attitude, you deserve to be thrown out . . . and you might be.

Plan the story as much as you can beforehand. Particularly for a feature, it is helpful for a beginner to jot down a scenario which lists proposed shots and roughly the footage planned for each. You will almost certainly deviate some from the plan when you get into the actual shooting, because what best shows reality is what you want to shoot. But your advance planning can move you through the story faster, make for less editing later, save film and tell a better story.

Veteran newsfilm photographers often sketch out possible story approaches in their minds while driving to a news scene. If it's a fire at a location you are familiar with, you may be thinking of such things as which position should give the best establishing shot.

When working with a reporter or someone else as a team, get your signals straight in advance. WBZ-TV's Ed Dooks suggests:

> Talk over the story with your reporter. Know what your reporter is thinking. Conversely make sure your reporter knows what you are thinking. Pre-plan your story together and remain flexible, ready to change this pre-planning if the story content is better told another way. Most important to remember, if the photographer can't communicate with the reporter, how in the world do you both expect to communicate with the viewer?

At many stations, of course, the photographer is often also the reporter.

Drive with Care

Conducting yourself professionally includes driving station vehicles (or your own) carefully and considerately. As News Director Ray Miller has put it for his KPRC-TV, Houston, staff:

> Drive courteously and defensively. If you have an accident, be as polite and helpful to the other party as possible. Make sure the police are called and a proper report is made for the police records. File your own report, with full details and names and particulars, with the news director at the earliest opportunity.
>
> We want to get to the scene of the action as soon as possible, but we do not want to hurt anyone on the way. If you should get involved in an accident on the way to an assignment, be sure to report it at once to the news director by two-way radio, so he can assign someone else to the story while you stay at the accident scene as long as necessary.

In parking at a news scene, be aware that you must get out again. Don't let your vehicle get trapped in by police or fire apparatus, spectators, or anything else which could prevent you from returning quickly to the station.

Access

Problems of access are also treated in Miller's KPRC-TV staff manual:

> There may be times when law enforcement agencies will try to deny news reporters access to the scene of a crime, plane crash or accident. The FBI, in plane crashes, may sometimes give local lawmen the impression that they are to keep everybody out, and this is sometimes construed to mean everybody including newsmen.
>
> If you are denied access to what you have been sent to cover, make the assignment desk aware of it at once. The desk will advise you how to proceed.
>
> But, in general, your best course is to find out who the senior local law enforcement officer present is and introduce yourself and tell him what you want. If he is under the impression that some federal agency has taken charge, you should appeal to his pride in his own authority and ask him how that can be. He can get you in, once you convince him it is the sensible thing for him to do.
>
> Get there any way you can. Your job is to get there and get the story. It is not your job to seek or create confrontations. The news director will defend you any time you resist unwarranted interference. But never get into physical combat with peace officers.
>
> If an officer detains you, make him tell you whether you are under arrest. If you are under arrest, go with him peacefully, and we will make the appropriate protest at the appropriate time. If you are not under arrest and there is any way you can get around the officer and get to the story you are seeking, that is what you should do.

Keep in mind, too, that some officers are more flexible than others. If there are alternate checkpoints and you fail to get in at one, try another.

You'll also probably have a better chance if you are known and respected by the local officers. The more personal contacts you can develop, the better. But keep them on a professional level. Never imply to a news source that any favors or special treatment can be expected from you or your station. If that happens, you will be on the way to losing the respect of everyone, including the news source.

Professional Conduct

Along with characteristics already mentioned, the professional gets to the assignment on time, works as unobtrusively as possible, and is always courteous and considerate of people involved in the news. From your behavior, people at a news scene draw impressions of your station and the profession of television journalism. Let them be favorable impressions.

It is unfortunate that network and large station crews sometimes are apparently unable to film a newsmaker in the walk between a car and a building without looking like a small mob. Crowding or jostling to get in close on someone cannot always be avoided, but it tends to make journalistic practitioners appear to be boors. Broadcast and print photographers and reporters, when seen in action on television, too often look like packs of animals pouncing on a prey. Of course, it's competitive and you cannot let your station be crowded out of the coverage. But do your best to show good manners to co-workers and the people in the news.

Think twice before shoving a camera or microphone into the face of a grief-stricken next-of-kin. Sometimes the privacy of a person in grief should take priority over the emotional film which the public supposedly wants to see. It's a decision you must make, and it varies according to the situation, but the professional is a human being who consider other people's feelings as well as the public's curiosity.

At the same time, don't be shy about your job. In most cases, if you need a closeup, move in for it. You are there doing a job for the television public, who like to see people and things up close, and most newsmakers don't mind.

Using common sense can reduce the film reporter's obtrusiveness in many situations. For example, routine shots of an attentive audience listening to a speaker all may be taken at one point early in the speech. Then the lights can be turned away from the audience, who can concentrate on the speaker without being bothered by your lights. Repeatedly turning the lights on the audience is not only distracting and discourteous, but largely unnecessary.

Be especially unobtrusive and well mannered if permitted to film in a courtroom or legislative chamber. Access to this kind of news is difficult enough without uncivilized camera reporters making matters worse. Television journalism is not helped by the camera crews who reportedly scarred furniture and burned cigarette holes in table tops of a U.S. Senate committee room.

Other standards of professional conduct are included in the RTNDA Code of Broadcast News Ethics (see Appendix).

Finally, don't promise anybody anything. Someone may want to know when the film will be on. But you have no way of knowing for sure when or even if it will be on. And if someone inquires about obtaining leftover film or a still picture blowup from a movie frame, refer the person to the news director. It is not for the photographer or reporter to commit the newsroom in any way.

Stick to Reality

Surveys show that television is a primary source of news for most Americans and that they trust it more than other news media. This is further reason for you to be trustworthy in camera-reporting what the viewers assume is reality. Some stations have encountered problems with the Federal Communications Commission for allegedly deceptive newsfilm practices. Federal regulations aside, you violate the public's trust if you make anything look different from the way it really was. Do not re-create, stage or alter news events even if such would help the film story. Our profession is journalism, not show business.

Be a Reporter

In many operations, newsfilm photographers often go out alone on stories and thus must handle the fact-gathering as well as shooting the film. And those who are accompanied by a separate reporter should think of themselves as part of a camera-*reporting* team.

Bring back all information which may be needed for the story. Get all identifications and other details which might conceivably be needed. Pick up any news releases, printed programs or speech texts. It is much easier to do this news gathering while at the scene than to get on ·the phone later to try to track down information which your news director demands that you deliver. In case you do need to call for further information, get the name and phone number of a good source while at the scene.

Unless absolutely certain that everything in the film is self explanatory, "slate" shots on a notepad as you shoot. It's all too easy to forget which labor leader was the one in the first closeup and which in the second. On most stories, such notes for a "poop sheet" can be jotted down between shooting. It's a good investment of time, one which differentiates camera reporters from mere picture takers.

Getting the story is the job of the camera reporter. Ed Dooks of WBZ-TV sums it up:

> What do you film when you are at a story? Because of the limited amount of time television allows for each story, we are essentially doing mini-mini-documentaries. A documentary of from one to four minutes of air time. A brief glimpse into the world of someone else. This glimpse has a start, body and ending. We have to decide what highlights of the world of someone else will best tell the story. Before shooting, put yourself in the seat of the viewer and ask yourself, "If I were there, what would I want to see that will tell me what I need to know about this story?" And then shoot just that.

Dooks also suggests that you save a little film at the end of a roll in case an unexpected good shot becomes available as you are leaving. After each assignment, Dooks reloads his cameras before driving to the next one. As he puts it, "You never know what you might find around the corner."

Like many newspaper reporters, newsfilm photographers sometimes degenerate into hacks. They become blasé, too casual about their work, mechanical. Of this occupational hazard, Dooks says:

> If I am shooting the story for the 50th time, I try to do the best job I can. This means I will be hunting for that thing that is different about this story to set it apart from the other 49 that have already been aired. How many times have you heard photogs grumbling because they have to go to another crummy city council meeting or news conference? Well, they are getting paid to do just that. They are getting paid to do the best job they can. So why go out hating to do a job? Why not go out with a positive attitude and do the best you can on that particular story? You may discover you did it better than the last time.

Closeups

Once you have established the story, *move in on your subject.* Emotions register in the face, or even in hands or nervously shuffling feet shown close up. But they tend to go unnoticed in a wide shot. Closeups can also show hands on a machine performing a delicate task. And newsfilm editors appreciate the ease with which closeups help a story fit together.

Don't overuse extreme closeups of faces, the jumping nostril shots which have become clichés. Normally the full head should show, with a little space between its top and the frame.

Keep in mind that it's harder to maintain focus and contain action in a tight closeup.

Shoot One for Chromakey

Photographers at many stations must keep in mind that the program producer may want to open the story with newsfilm on Chromakey, an electronic process which places the image of film or other visuals on the screen with the newscaster. Since the center of attention in the film should not be blocked by the newscaster, shoot an appropriately framed shot or two for potential use as a Chromakey establisher. Center the attention in the film frame away from where the newscaster will be sitting, for example, in the right-hand half of the frame.

KTRK-TV, Houston, News Director Walt Hawver has instructed his photographers:

TO SHOOT ONE FOR CHROMAKEY means to include an establishing shot so composed that its main point of interest is not blocked out by the newscaster if the film is "keyed" onto the screen. On the WMTV, Madison, Wis., news set (top) only a blue backdrop is ever seen behind Tom Milbourn. But on the television screen (bottom) Chromakey can electronically replace the image of the backdrop with a scene from a news story.

Remember on the spot of the story that a freeze frame or 5-second tease for Chromakey may be asked for and shoot it accordingly. Some Chromas automatically suggest themselves—the sign outside a bank that has been robbed, the raging fire, the face of a principal in the story. There are stories where it is impossible to think of framing shots off center, but these are few and far between.

Be sure also to shoot a regularly framed establishing shot in case Chromakey is not used, as will often be the case.

TYPES OF STORIES

Newsfilm photographers in most operations get a variety of assignments on the average day. You may go from an early morning fire to the mayor's news conference to strike picketing to a speech and, on the way in, shoot some weather film. Many types of stories have already been mentioned in connection with general techniques. Special consideration will be given a few which either pose particular problems or are among those most often covered.

Accidents and Fires

If possible, get a wide shot establishing the location of an accident or fire. Photographers are sometimes so preoccupied with what's flaming that they forget to show it in the context of neighboring buildings. Similarly, they tend to become so absorbed in wreckage that they may fail to show the full general scene where an auto collision or plane crash took place.

Accident film is normally rather static. About all you can usually show are effects—what's left. Skid marks help tell the story. And there are the obvious closeups of wreckage. Cutaways of spectators or investigating officers should also be filmed. Policies vary, but most stations do not show corpses or badly mangled accident victims. The issue is not so much whether home viewers may be offended as whether you are being properly considerate of the victims and their next of kin.

Fire film can be spectacular. But remember that firefighters and spectators are as much part of the story as the flames. The real drama usually lies in the contest between the firefighters and the fire. And seeing spectators helps the viewer become a spectator. People relate to the news when they see other people in your film.

Give top priority to getting shots of people while they are available. When arriving at the scene, check at once to see if injured victims or witnesses are still there. They will probably be gone from the scene long before the wrecked car or burning building.

GETTING TO KNOW fire and police department personnel can enhance cooperation. In Houston they all know James Priest of KTRK.

HELMETS are sometimes advisable gear in filming civil disorders. Ed Dooks shoots sound-on-film and Bill Franklin (left) "runs sound" for WBZ-TV in covering a Boston demonstration. Franklin is using a shotgun microphone covered with a windscreen.

Civil Disorder

In covering demonstrations or disturbances where emotions are high and violence is easily triggered, be as unobtrusive and detached as possible. KPRC-TV's Ray Miller advises his staff in a policy manual:

> We will use unmarked cars at the scene, avoid using additional lights, and generally avoid contributing to any disorder there may be.
> At such disturbances, newsmen sometimes identify with the police or others at the scene, reporting what takes place from the point of view of a participant rather than as an objective reporter. Channel 2 News is not to be identified with anyone present at the scene. We will do our best to be fair to all present.
> We will take no unnecessary personal risks and will obey the orders of the police at such disorders, even if they seem unreasonable. If what seem to be unreasonable orders are issued, appropriate action will be taken only by the news director or his representative after receipt of a full report. You may have to take some verbal abuse, but don't let yourself get drawn into an argument or a physical exchange.

For filming civil disorder, WBZ-TV, Boston, has a policy of using a "back up man"—a second photographer whose job is to watch out for the one who is filming. Thanks to such a "back up man," Ed Dooks says, his "head was saved from becoming part of the sidewalk during a riot."

No matter how strongly partisan you may feel as a private citizen, you must not let it affect your work. Remember that you are there not as a private citizen but as a representative of a television audience consisting of people of all points of view.

Standuppers

A standup report is one in which a reporter stands at the scene of a news event, looks at the camera and tells the story. In its pure form, the entire report is shot on the scene, and appropriately illustrative actuality film is often brought in as video from B-roll for part of the report. Quite often, however, only a "wraparound" of the reporter at the scene is filmed. That's the open, close or both. Then, back at the station, the reporter narrates the actuality film which serves as the heart of the story. This second approach can usually be spotted by the change in audio perspective when the reporter goes from field to studio and usually from one type of microphone to another. Some wild sound tape recorded at the news scene and played beneath the studio narration can help cover the abrupt audio change.

Get a story-telling background. Otherwise, you might as well shoot under ideal studio conditions back at the station. The state capitol, a legislative chamber, a classroom, a riot, holiday traffic or street construction are common backgrounds which can be effective for standuppers. By contrast, standing the reporter against a wall or other nondescript background contributes nothing. Also, avoid extremely bright backgrounds which may cause the TV chain's automatic shader to darken out the reporter's face in on-air projection.

It is often effective to establish a standupper with a wide shot, zoom in for a closeup of the reporter, and (later in editing) cut to

A STORY-TELLING BACKGROUND is important for a standup report. Pat Kleiman of WITI-TV, Milwaukee, chooses an appropriate location for a report on food prices.

A PROMPTER held just under the lens can free the on-camera reporter from having to look up and down from notes or a script. Karen Norman holds the prompter as Director of Communications Carl Zimmerman does an on-location editorial for WITI-TV, Milwaukee. Chief Photographer Bob Homberg operates the CP-16 camera from a sturdy tripod and uses earphones to monitor the sound. Note the windscreen on the microphone.

actuality film of the situation. This approach can be especially useful if the first shot of actuality film is a wide scene, since a visual jump cut is less likely to occur in cutting to a wide scene from a closeup than from another wide scene.

Standuppers can easily be overdone. Often the viewer would get more information from seeing the situation in the news rather than watching a reporter stand and talk about it.

Larrye deBear of WTIC-TV, Hartford, Conn., has these suggestions:

Standuppers should be used only if the content of the story is major enough to warrant it and only if the standup reporter has covered the story.

These reports can be done in one take straight through, provided the photographer varies his shots somewhat (from a medium to a closeup to a medium-closeup, for example). However, if a reporter feels he would like to pause once in awhile to check his notes, then the standupper can be done in takes. In each case, the photographer varies his shot, not within the take, but from take to take. And for smoother editing, the reporter, at the start of each take, should begin with the last few words of the previous take. This does away with lip flap in the editing process.

Interviews

Interviews—the most common source of TV's "talking heads"—
are usually shot over the shoulder of the interviewer and angled slightly
from head-on of the interviewee. As explained in Chapter 5, reversal
shots of the interviewer re-asking the questions are sometimes shot
following the interview and edited in for a two-camera effect. The resulting screen direction must be consistent. If the news source is
looking to the left in the interview footage, the reporter must be looking
to the right in the reversals.

When should you use the zoom? WBZ-TV's Ed Dooks advises:

> When your reporter asks a question of your talking head, this is the
> best time to zoom to change your shot. Now, to eliminate that zoom,
> shoot reverse angle cutaway questions after the interview is over, and
> back in the editing room cut those reverse angle questions in the place
> of the original questions and you now have an interview with no zooms,
> and it looks like it was shot with two cameras. . . . The only time I might
> zoom during an answer is if the person is saying something of such in-
> terest that it would naturally make me *lean in closer* to hear what is
> being said.

Because the re-shooting of interview questions as SOF reversals
may be considered "staging," and they often look it, many stations use
them sparingly if at all. Alternatives are available. If the purpose of a
reversal is to cover a visual jump cut, the job can be done better by a
silent film cutaway on B-roll (a second projector providing video while
audio continues from the main A-roll projector). Or a voice-over para-
phrase of the question may be used behind silent or natural SOF as a
substitute for the SOF question. Actually, watching the interviewee
listening to a short question is sometimes an effective shot in itself.
And if visual variety is needed for this approach, an appropriate B-roll
cutaway or cut-in of either or both persons may be run. Just go easy on
reversals. They are poorly used or overused by some stations.

While over-the-shoulder is generally the most effective angle for
shooting an interview, look for opportunities to use other approaches occasionally and thus break the pattern of the standard technique.
Especially if conditions make it difficult to shoot effective reversals (and
skip ineffective ones, because they look terribly staged!), you may try
standing the reporter and the news source facing each other, with the
interviewee slightly angled toward the camera. Airport and locker room
interviews may lend themselves to this setup. But often a better solution
in tight quarters is simply to forget about showing the reporter and film
a closeup of the news source's face as the viewer would see it in normal
conversation.

OVER-THE-SHOULDER of the reporter is often the best position for filming an interview. In shooting this one over Jill Geisler's shoulder, Jim Pluta of WITI-TV, Milwaukee, shoulder-balances the camera. Tripods are seldom feasible for fast-moving stories such as fires.

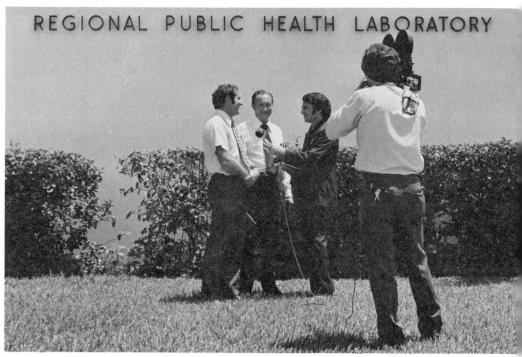

SIDE-BY-SIDE positions are sometimes used, particularly when more than one person is interviewed at the same time. Two Dade County health officials are interviewed by Bob Mayer as Warren Jones films for a WTVJ, Miami, series which investigated restaurant kitchen cleanliness.

If possible, impose a "no smoking" rule on interviews. Editing problems can result when there is smoke in the air or a cigarette at the lips in one shot but not in the next.

If positioning permits the reporter to see you, give cues as you near the end of the film available. This will be just under 11 minutes for a full 400-foot magazine. Finger cues can indicate 3, 2, 1, ½ and no minutes to go.

Speeches

Tripod-mounted SOF cameras are used for most speech coverage, and for good reason. The speaker is seen in relation to a stationary podium which makes any shakiness of a shoulder-braced camera conspicuous.

In part to avoid unnecessary distraction, get there early and set up cameras and lights in advance if possible. In rooms with dimensions permitting, the SOF camera and key light are often set up to one side at about a 30-45 degree angle to the speaker, the fill light going on the opposite side, and possibly a back light in the front corner on the camera side. The microphone may need taping for secure positioning on the podium.

For editing purposes, shoot establishing shots and cutaways. A silent camera is often used for this, but if this shooting can be done with natural SOF, that's even better.

Be selective in your shooting. Most budgets do not permit filming entire speeches, and most of the film would go unused anyway. If you are limited to 400 feet (11 minutes), for example, on a 45-minute speech, the problem is which 11 minutes to shoot. Try for an advance copy of the speech and mark the excerpts to be shot. Or by talking with the speaker or a press aide in advance, you may get an indication of when what you want will be coming up. Some speakers, for example, public officials who have become familiar with the needs of TV, may even be willing to give you a signal when that portion is coming up.

Otherwise, play it by ear. In general, the first part of a speech is throwaway, the middle can provide good material, and the best nut-shelling (and sometimes bombshelling) for TV excerpts often comes near the end. Try to save at least 100 feet for some highly news-pegged comments the speaker may tack on unexpectedly at the end.

Keep in mind, too, that a speaker who says nothing new in the speech may provide good material in response to questions from the audience or from an enterprising reporter.

News Conferences

Since news conferences are set up for the convenience of the news media, selective shooting is easier there than during an unscripted speech. The questions being asked will cue you as to whether the topic is one you want to use film on. Stopping and starting the camera during questions is acceptable, since sound pickup from questioners is usually inferior and your audience wants to hear and see the newsmaker's answer, not the reporter's question.

Setting up camera and lights is done much as for speeches, except that the room will probably be smaller and there will be more flexibility for positioning your equipment.

Again, shoot cutaways. But avoid the clichéd closeups of note taking and cameras running. Try long shots of the group of reporters, a closeup of the mayor's administrative assistant, or even experiment with something original, difficult as that may be in news conference settings.

Governmental Proceedings

Newsfilm cameras are barred from most courtrooms and all too many legislative chambers. If you are granted access, leave a positive impression. Otherwise, still another door may be closed to what Chief Justice Earl Warren once called television's "all-seeing eye."

In states where courtroom television coverage is not flatly prohibited, it is usually left up to the judge. Restricted filming is sometimes permitted. For example, you may be permitted to shoot during recesses or as long as you don't show certain witnesses or other principals who may object. The judge is in charge of the courtroom and is to be obeyed on these and all other matters. Violations can send you to jail for contempt of court.

Unless TV coverage of legislative proceedings is expressly permitted, you may bring in and use your equipment only at the pleasure of the official body, which often delegates such decisions to the presiding officer. If told by this person not to shoot, don't. If you feel the order was unjust, let your news director do the fighting for access.

Either be unobtrusive or keep out of judicial or legislative chambers. Don't bring in a noisy camera. If your station will not invest in quiet-running equipment, representatives of your station do not deserve access.

Even if a helpful judge permits it, don't bring photo lights into a courtroom. They are unnecessary with the film and lenses now available. Color and depth of field may be less than ideal, but the film should still be of adequate quality, and you will not be inviting television's exclusion on grounds of distraction. Similarly, for legislative proceedings, get by on existing light if possible. The sooner TV news can shed its image of a bunch of "producers" turning everything into a brilliantly lighted studio, the more stories will be open to our cameras.

In some states, additional lights have been installed in legislative chambers to facilitate more effective newsfilming by existing light. In North Dakota, for example, the extra lights were put in after three years of spadework by television news representatives working with the state's legislative council. The West Virginia Legislature installed new House chamber lighting when color television came along, requiring higher light levels. This was accomplished because broadcast journalists convinced lawmakers the public would get a distorted view of a gloomy setting without proper lighting. RTNDA members have traditionally been among the leaders in efforts toward such progress in the television news coverage of governmental proceedings.

Features

In shooting a feature, you are usually showing a situation or process rather than an event. Therefore, it is efficient and no real violation of reality to plot out the story and even do some setting up of certain shots. Such pre-planning can save film and make for a better feature. At the same time, while some arranging is acceptable, avoid any action that might be construed as "staging," especially if a possible illegality is involved in what you are shooting. Having a blacksmith shoe a horse for the convenience of your camera is no problem if that's the way he normally shoes them anyway. But do not let anyone set up an illegal crap game for your camera, even if the gathering looks exactly like the ones held when television is not there.

Investigative Reporting

Using a camera as a tool for investigative reporting can be difficult and even dangerous. To show a bookie joint in operation, police officers taking payoffs, a nursing home giving inhuman treatment to the elderly, or a powerful landlord's housing violating city standards requires ingenuity and intestinal fortitude as well as photographic and reportorial skill. But such use of newsfilm can be television's greatest public service. This is journalism which goes beyond the all too common use of film merely to illustrate for television what has already been reported elsewhere.

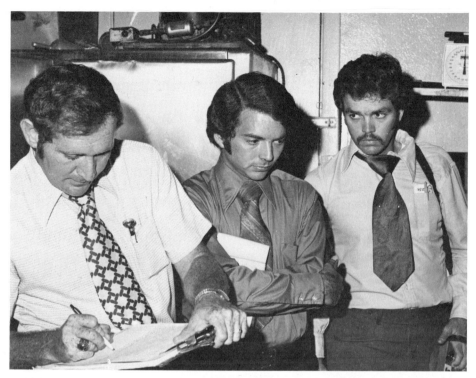

INVESTIGATIVE REPORTING is often done by teams of TV journalists. Reporter Bob Mayer (center) and photographer Warren Jones (right) of WTVJ, Miami, accompanied restaurant inspectors into kitchens for a "Not on the Menu" series concerning kitchen sanitation.

The filming will often be done under adverse conditions. There may be no choice but to use available light. Close quarters may require imaginative angling even with a wide angle lens. You may have to find a way to shoot reasonably steady film with a telephoto lens without a tripod. And you may need an unobtrusive microphone.

Good investigative and enterprise reporting requires an investment of personnel time and effort which many stations consider too expensive.

A station doing this kind of reporting must have its attorney constantly available to check legally ticklish aspects of the story and to help determine whether certain things should be filmed or reported.

Finally, investigative reporting requires the full support of a news director and station manager who are not afraid of rocking boats, if necessary, in the public interest.

DOCUMENTARIES

Most principles of filming regular length news stories are even more applicable to documentaries. Special attention must be given continuity, pacing and other elements of story telling. Or you will not be able to sustain viewer interests for the 10, 30, 60 or more minutes which a documentary segment or program may run.

Some topics lend themselves better to film documentation than do others. If the topic is the conflicting philosophies of politicians or others, a simple, inexpensive, in-studio panel discussion may serve as well as a so-called documentary which consists only of a series of talking heads. The most effective documentaries use film to show situations—poverty, environmental waste, school problems, how tax dollars are used and misused, the everyday life of a popular singer or athlete, or the state of noise pollution.

It's easier if your subjects are interesting people who express basic feelings in a natural way. Migrant workers, musicians, truck drivers and students are among those who usually make interesting film. Public officials, business executives and professors are among the subjects who are often significant but also often dull. This does not mean that they are to be avoided, only that you keep such factors in mind in planning and pacing a documentary. No matter how significant the content, if it puts the viewer to sleep, communication fails.

Research is essential. A thorough reporting job should be done before filming begins. Through interviews, observation, newspapers, books and other sources, familiarize yourself with all aspects of the situation to be filmed. Only then will you be able to make the decisions needed for effective documentation.

Plan the filming. Visualize potential film as it would fit together to make the needed points. Rough it all out on paper in what is sometimes called a scenario—scenes, sound segments and their times as they might be used in the documentary. There will be changes, probably many of them, when you start shooting. You must not permit a scenario to interfere with your reporting the situation in the truest possible way. But this advance planning enables you to focus on the main elements, to save film and time, and to tell the story better.

Be selective. Don't overload the viewer with too many different aspects or details of the situation. Decide which elements are most important and then treat them thoroughly. Make a few points well. Too much moving from one point to another tends to confuse the viewer.

Continuity is essential. Each scene, interview or other ingredient of the documentary must lead logically to the next. And the whole report must fit together to leave the viewer with an integral overall impression at the end. The viewer may feel enlightened, angered, motivated to action, or even entertained. But if the documentary lacks continuity, the final impression will more likely be—what was that all about?

Pacing can help reduce yawning and dial-twisting. If you are heavy on film of significant but dull speakers, try to break up their segments with footage which carries some excitement. To put sound film of several city officials together in one block and film of angry citizens in another block of the documentary will invite monotony. If the film permits going back and forth between officials and citizens, this will probably enhance pacing and interest.

Natural sound is usually needed. Silent film soon becomes boring. Besides, if your goal is true documentation, such a vital part of reality as sound can hardly be left out.

B-roll should normally be a part of any documentary in which people talk about situations or conditions. There is no better place to see, for example, traffic hazards or dirty restaurant kitchens than when news sources are talking about them. B-roll film may also be used to cover lip flap and other editing flaws which might be tolerable in the small dosage of a regular length story but distracting and annoying when appearing at several points in a documentary.

Double-system is recommended for the smoothest editing. Some stations which do not normally use double-system sound for daily newsfilm use it for documentaries, which usually allow more time for the complex editing which double-system can involve.

Ideally, people shown doing things in a documentary will be going about those activities as if the camera were not there. It may help to set up for shooting and then let them proceed with the activity for awhile before actual filming begins. This permits the initial camera awareness to wear off and the people to be shown concentrating on their activity instead of their appearance on television.

Unless a reporter is to be shown doing interviews through the documentary, microphones should be kept out of pictures as much as possible. They call attention to TV's presence. Using a boom, shotgun or lavalier mike instead of a hand mike may be the solution.

Keep your filming honest and unpretentious. Big cinematographic productions with arty shots and strained gimmicks tend to bedazzle at the expense of reporting. Imaginative approaches are needed, and a documentary permits you to use whatever talent you have for film reporting. Just let your every effort be directed at telling the story in the most effective way. The story must dictate film techniques, not vice versa. When you use a camera for television newsfilm or documentary, you are not "making" a film. You are "using" film as a tool to document reality.

REMINDERS

- Before leaving for a story, be sure you have all equipment needed.
- Tag malfunctioning equipment to keep someone else from losing a story with it.
- In cold climates, keep cameras and batteries warm.
- When possible, plan your story before you shoot it.
- Park your car where you can get out easily.
- Use tact, good sense and ingenuity to get the story.
- Do not re-create, stage or alter news events for your camera.
- Bring back all information which may be needed to script the story.
- Slate shots as needed to make identifications clear.
- Save a little film for the unexpected good shot at the end.
- Compose an establishing shot for Chromakey if your station has it.
- In filming accidents, fires, other spot news and features, get shots of people.
- In filming civil disorder, be as unobtrusive as possible.
- Shoot standuppers in front of story-telling backgrounds.
- Most interviews are best shot over the shoulder of the reporter.
- If the news source is looking to the left in interview footage, the reporter must be looking to the right in reversals.
- Try to get an advance text when covering speeches.
- Shoot lots of cutaways at speeches and news conferences.
- Don't use noisy equipment in covering a legislative or judicial session.
- Don't promise anybody anything.
- Continuity, pacing and other elements of newsfilm story telling are especially important in documentaries.

7 | Editing Newsfilm

Shooting and editing newsfilm are so closely related that it is unrealistic to treat them as distinctly separate processes. The survey conducted for this book showed that in at least half the TV newsrooms, most editing was being done by photographers. Whether or not you are a photographer who edits film regularly, some experience at the editing table will help you to shoot newsfilm which will require less editing.

Editing film consists of viewing it and then doing whatever is required to turn it into an effective story of the desired length. This usually involves cutting (breaking) and joining (splicing) parts of the film to remove shots, shorten them or change their sequence. If a sound track is used, you must consider the sound as well as the picture at each step.

When the film has been edited to fit together the way you wish, it is delivered on a reel to the station's control room, where a projectionist puts it on a film chain, a machine which projects it for transmission as part of a television signal to the home set.

Two reels of newsfilm may be rolled on projectors at the same time, permitting sound from one reel to be used with picture from the other. One is called the A-roll and the other the B-roll. For example, while we listen to a news source's description of a situation from the

A-roll sound track, we may see film of the situation from the B-roll. Editing for such effects can be complex.

As elsewhere in newsfilm, learn to walk before trying to run. First, master the mechanics of basic equipment. Next, learn to edit silent film. Then, move to the editing of A-roll sound film, and finally, to synchronized A-roll and B-roll editing and even double-system editing if your station has facilities for this technique.

Because in-camera editing is part of shooting, many points made for the photographer in Chapters 3 and 6 apply equally for the editor in this chapter. A few of the main ones will be referred to again.

WHY EDIT?

If there is one major fault in editing, it is that not enough of it is done. Many films run too long. Stop and consider the percentage of time allotted to any film story compared to the total newscast time and see if you can justify that much emphasis for the story, aside from the fact that it was on film. Trimmed of second rate or unnecessary footage, stories not only take less time but make their points more effectively.

The purposes of editing are 1) to remove unwanted film and 2) to rearrange what is left to tell the story in the best possible way.

Film may be unwanted because of bad quality. Focus may be fuzzy or soft. The film may be too dark or too light (under- or over-exposed). It may be shaky—perhaps the photographer hand-held with a 2-inch lens. If film is not sharp, properly exposed and reasonably steady, *throw it out!* One bad shot can ruin the effect of an otherwise excellent film story.

There are exceptions, of course. Even if its quality were not ideal, you would certainly want to use dramatic, story-telling film of a night-time prison riot or plane crash. The home viewer understands that such film is often shot under adverse conditions. But do not inflict soft, dark or shaky film of a feature or a visually routine city council meeting upon the viewer. Such film is not vital enough to justify its use when quality is bad.

Film of perfectly good quality is often thrown out because there is too much of it. Shots may be too long or too similar. Or they may not contribute enough to the story to justify their use.

Rearranging the order of shots or sequences may give a better flow. For example, logistics may have caused the establisher to be shot in mid-reel, or cutaways may need to be moved around.

EQUIPMENT

A TV news operation should have at least two or three complete editing rigs, or work stations. For editing silent or single-system sound film, recommended equipment includes:

Editing table. Most stations have them custom-made. Some of the ready-made commercial products are overpriced and poorly designed. There must be counter space for all equipment, and everything should be within normal arm's reach.

Film bin. Loose film hangs into this container while being edited. The bin may be a separate flannel-lined basket on wheels or part of the editing table as an enclosed recess about three feet across at the rear of the table. On a board mounted horizontally a foot or so above the bin, will be one or two rows of clips from which strips of film may be hung.

Splicer. This device for joining one piece of film to another should be fast-acting, requiring no more than 10 seconds of setting time for a splice to "take." Cement splicers come in cold or hot (electrically heated) models. Hot splicers like the Maier-Hancock are the most common, though some editors prefer splicers which use Mylar tape instead of cement.

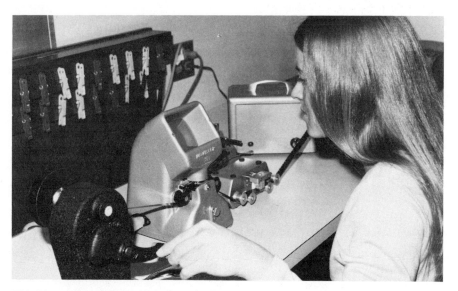

EDITING SINGLE-SYSTEM SOUND film for WISC-TV, Madison, University of Wisconsin broadcast journalism student Laura Raun hand-winds the magnetic-striped film through a viewer and (just to the right of it) a sound reader. The sound is heard from a speaker (with handle on top) in the background. If the rewind is turned at roughly 24 frames per second, the sound is intelligible. Short film segments hang from flexible plastic clothespins into a film bin which is part of the custom-built editing table.

A FILM VIEWER such as the much-used Moviscop gives a sharp, bright image and can be used effectively in a normally lighted room.

A HOT SPLICER receiving proper maintenance makes fast, strong splices. A film end is first locked into the righthand section, which is then raised back out of the way while the other film end is locked into the left section. A blade in the middle is used to scrape emulsion from between two frames of the film on the left. Cement is applied with a brush to the scraped area, and the right-hand section is promptly brought back down. Within a few seconds the two ends are spliced firmly together, and the film can be disengaged. Splicers should be kept free of dried cement at all times.

A SYNCHRONIZER, which is a multi-ganged film timer, is used for A-B roll editing. The two reels of film will be run on projectors at the same time, permitting the simultaneous use of sound from one film and picture from the other. The precision timing needed for going back and forth between reels for sound or picture is best done with a synchronizer, which keeps film for the two reels running through at exactly the same rate. Points where roll-through leader is to be spliced into a reel are marked.

Viewer. As film is wound, usually manually, through this device, the picture is shown on its small glass screen. Viewers such as the Zeiss Moviscop give a sharp, bright image in a normally lighted room. The most commonly used viewers are made primarily for prints (which have the emulsion on the underside of the film), not for TV's reversal film (which is always emulsion up after processing). This means that, for an upright image, the TV newsfilm editor must run the film from left to right to put the emulsion down, and then flip the film over for every splice. Many editors feel that efficiency is increased by using the less common and generally a little more expensive viewers which are made for the right-to-left operation which is natural for reversal film.

Rewinds. One is mounted on each side of the viewer. With a handle in each hand, the operator may run the film back and forth through the viewer, timer and sound reader. Rewinds attached to the viewer tend to be shaky. They are best mounted permanently to the table top. Often an electric motor is attached to one side for rewinding full reels.

Film timer. Timing may be by feet or seconds of film. Footage counters require a conversion to time (3 feet equal 5 seconds for 16mm film running at TV speed of 24 frames for second). Timers which register directly in seconds and minutes are usually preferred. The timer for most A-B roll or double-system editing must be a *synchronizer* with "gangs" (sprocketed wheels) to time more than one reel of film simultaneously.

Sound reader. When film is run through this little device, usually fed manually by the rewinds, the sound track passes over a pickup head which is wired to an amplifier-speaker. With a little practice, the editor gets the feel for turning the rewind handle at the roughly 24 fps rate necessary for intelligible sound. Fast winding and rewinding, easy and precise back and forth movement and marking of film, and the absence of threading make the sound reader easier to use than a projector for SOF editing. The reader can be attached directly to the film timer for added convenience.

Projector. This gives the bigger look at unedited or edited film. Like the sound reader, it must have a magnetic pickup head for the magnetic sound tracks which are standard for TV.

Supplies. These include: film cement or Mylar editing tape, film cleaner, white lintless cotton gloves, ½-inch masking tape, leader (opaque film which is put on the head and tail of film), numerous reels of various sizes (especially 100 and 400 foot), plastic cores for storing film without reels, one or two split reels (necessary for working with film on cores), and a small but strong magnet for erasing tails of magnetic SOF. A roomy wastebasket should be nearby for rejected film. Don't throw it on "the cutting-room floor."

PROCEDURE

First, don't do unnecessary editing. A good photographer often brings in film that requires little if any cutting. Most stories can be improved at the editing table, it's true, but don't feel that you must chop every story to pieces and splice it back together again. Utilize in-camera editing which has already been done.

Steps

The steps in editing *silent* film vary by stations and equipment, but usually are roughly as follows:

1) *View the film* to see what you have to work with. Putting it on a projector is recommended for the beginner, though a veteran can usually do as well with the table viewer. Keep in mind that most tele-viewing is done in rooms with normal lighting, and viewer bulbs tend to give very bright pictures. If much dimming is necessary for you to see what is on the film, it is probably too dark to use.

2) *Decide which shots* to use and in what order. Do this by running the film back and forth through the viewer until you can pretty well visualize how the finally edited story will look. Run it through easily and no more often than necessary, or it may pick up scratches. This viewing and decision-making should precede any film cutting. You may want to time certain shots, and this is easier before the film has been cut into pieces. With practice, you can estimate gross film time without running it through a timer at this stage of editing. You'll pick up little time-savers. For example, for many people, a full sideways extension of an arm puts the film in that hand 4 feet from the viewer lamp. The two rewinds likely will be about 3 feet apart.

3) *Cut the film.* Actually, just break it. Television editors seldom use scissors on 16mm film. It snaps easily from the perforated edge. Going from head to tail of the unedited film, break it where necessary. Throw out film you know you will not want. If in doubt, put it aside on an end-of-the row clip or a special reel. Hang film in the order of planned use, from left to right being best for most editors, on the row of clips. Reels may work better than clips for longer film cuts, as in SOF editing.

Beware of stray frames, the one or two remaining frames you did not intend to use but which were accidentally left at the end of an adjoining shot which you are using. Cutting just inside rather than exactly at the end of the shot you are using is a precaution against those stray frames which will flash on almost subliminally.

An example of how cutting might go for a silent film story needing more than average editing:

The first shot on the roll is light struck, so it and the leader go into the waste bin. Shots #2 and #3 will be used in sequence about midway in the story and are hung in one piece about midway in the row of clips. Shot #4 is your establisher but you want only 4 of the 8 feet, so you break off the 4 feet you like best and hang it on clip #1 and throw out the leftover. Shot #5 is a bit soft—into the waste bin! Shots #6 and #7, with a bit of trimming, are to follow the establisher in order. Snap a foot or two off the front of #6 and the tail of #7 and hang the rest on clip #2. Shots #8 and #9 duplicate each other. You choose #9 and hang it on clip #3. You see a possibility that you may also want #8, so you hang it on a reserve clip at the end of the row instead of throwing it out just now. (Never throw it out if there's a chance you may need it.) Shots #10 and #11 are in sequence with #9 and remain attached to #9, though #11 is a bit long and you snap a foot or two off the end of it. Shot #12 is shaky and is thrown out. A smooth flowing newsfilm story should now be hanging from left to right, ready for splicing.

Caution! During cutting and all other film handling, either wear white lintless cotton gloves or learn to handle the film by its edges. By all means, keep your bare fingers off the emulsion. That's the less glossy of the two sides of film, the one on which the picture is, in effect, imprinted.

3a) *Optional rough-cut timing* may be done at this point. This means putting the film together with masking tape, running it through the viewer and timer to see that everything checks out, and adjusting as needed before any splicing is done. Skilled editors can often skip this step because adjustments will so seldom be needed. In some stations the rough-cut approach is necessary because splicing is permitted only by unionized splice-makers who are not part of the news department.

4) *Splice the film* story together. Start with the leader your station specifies, splicing it to the head of the first shot. Then splice the tail of this strip of film to the head of the second strip, etc. Some leader should also be spliced to the tail of the story.

The process will not be detailed here, since splicer manuals are easy to follow, but a few suggestions are in order.

In making cement splices, be sure the emulsion is smoothly and evenly scraped all the way across. If you snag a performation, start all over at the next undamaged frame.

Apply the cement evenly across the scrape. Don't use heavy globs, but be sure the scraped area is fully covered.

Bring the top part of the splicer down firmly in a single stroke, but don't slam it.

Test the splice by feeling to see that it is not rough edged and by applying mild pressure. Don't pull hard or the new splice may break or be weakened.

If a splice is imperfect, do it over—at least a frame down into both shots, *not* on the old scrape.

Keep the splicer clean as you go. Some editors have a habit of wiping each cutting edge with a stroke of a lintless cloth as soon as it is disengaged after each splice. Never use a hard object to remove gummed cement from a splicer. A cloth soaked with film cleaner or alcohol will soften it for easy wiping off.

A strong splice in magnetic SOF requires an extra step—removing the stripes of magnetic tape where the cement is to be applied. The tape won't weld. It can be removed by the splicer's scraper after flipping the film over and locking it in the required position. The tape can also be scraped away with a razor blade or emery board applied to the underside of the film while it is locked normally in the splicer, but be careful not to scrape the splicer surface. A third method is to dab the tape stripes with film cement, which instantly melts them, and then wipe this off while the film is locked normally in the splicer. This tends to get messy.

5) *Slate shots or sequences* and note their footage or time as needed for precise script matching and cueing. The amount needed will vary by stories.

6) *Adjust length as needed.* If the rough-cut procedure is used, part or all of this will have been done earlier.

7) *Clean the film.* There is no separate work print to mess up in TV news. The film edited is the film shown, so handle it with care. Wind the film through a lint-free pad or glove which has been dampened with cleaning fluid and is held between thumb and fingers. Then rewind it for at least one dry cleaning through another lint-free pad or glove.

As the film runs through your fingers in the cleaning process, keep them alert for any defect such as a broken perforation or a rough splice. If you feel a snag or bump as the film runs through your hand, stop and check it. Now, not airtime, is the time to detect a bad splice.

In winding and rewinding, be sure the film comes off one reel and goes on the other reel in the same way—either over the reel for both left and right sides or under the reel for both. If the film comes off from under one roll but goes on from over the other, emulsion and perforations will be on the wrong side for normal projection.

Keep good tension on the film during this process. TV film chain projectors tend to put heavy stress on the film. If a splice won't hold under stress between the editing rewinds, it probably won't make it on the chain projector.

8) *Label* the film with masking tape placed on the head of the leader of the ready-to-go reel of film.

9) *Dispose of outtakes,* the unused but usable film hanging on the reserve clips. Either throw them out or, if there's a chance they may ever be needed, splice or tape them together on an appropriately labelled reel. Do *not* leave any film hanging or lying around to be in the way for the next story.

10) *Clean up* everything. Clean the splicer, brush any film scraps off the table top, and make sure the viewer lamp is turned off. Follow the old military rule of leaving all equipment ready for the next user.

FILM LANGUAGE

Newsfilm editing should be done by a television journalist who understands both news values and the language of film. There are no magic formulas and few rules. Learning film language is largely an individual process of developing an awareness of the ways scenes and images can fit together to communicate reality. Well edited film can convey moods and feelings—of rushing flood waters, a hot day, despair in a ghetto, hostility in a confrontation, excitement at a rock concert, relief at the end of a political campaign.

An editor looking at unedited film visualizes the many ways shots can go together and chooses the combination which tells the story best, while always preserving the integrity of the news story. Never should an editor distort a film report of an event simply to make a more "interesting" story.

Establishing Shots

As discussed in Chapter 3, the establishing shot should draw interest and cue the viewer to the type of story. This usually includes establishing location and thus is most often a long shot (LS) rather than medium (MS) or closeup (CU) in perspective. Examples:

> —LS building in flames, showing its relationship to neighboring buildings.
> —LS from rear of audience at music festival.
> —LS state prison with identifying sign in foreground.

If the opening shot is to be Chromakeyed onto the screen with the newscaster, try to pick one in which the newscaster will not block out important action. As noted in Chapter 6, many photographers are instructed routinely to shoot for Chromakey, by including at least one potential establisher with main action confined, for example, to the right-hand half or upper right-hand quarter of the frame.

Length of Shots

The opening shot should run long enough to establish the story but not long enough to start boring. Silent film establishers often run 3-4 feet (5-7 seconds), but a very simple shot may run shorter. Those with natural sound may run longer.

Except for certain montages, a shot should remain on the screen long enough for the viewer to take in the scene's basic information but not much longer. One showing a wide area may need to be held for more time than a closeup because it contains more to be assimilated for meaningful viewing. A shot which introduces something new normally needs to be held longer than one we have seen before.

A shot of a sign normally should run as long as it takes to leisurely read the words which most people would want to read. If "Franklin, Pop. 6247" flashes on the screen for only 2 seconds, some viewers may be annoyed because they didn't quite have time to grasp what the sign said. But if it's held for more than 5 seconds, your audience may start yawning. Incidentally, 2 seconds would probably be enough for a "Stop" sign—that message gets through fast.

A variety of shots is usually needed, but too much jumping around with very short shots can give a choppy effect.

Short shots can also make action appear faster and more exciting. They tend to excite and stimulate, making the mind work faster. When visual excitement is what you want—as for a rock concert, sports event or fast-paced political campaigning—short, varied shots in abundance may be fine. But this type of editing tends to be incompatible with narration which demands close attention of the listener-viewer. The film draws so much attention that there is not enough left over for assimilating complex narration.

Conversely, shots which run longer tend to relax and let narration come through. They are recommended when the narration contains much essential information. Longer shots would be appropriate for the candidate relaxing at the end of a campaign or for a somber event such as a funeral.

Visual Continuity

Continuity from shot to shot is essential. The viewer should feel almost as if witnessing the event, unaware of editing or the fact that it's all on film. Marty Smith of Capital Film Laboratories has defined the basic premise of telling stories with film as "the special relationship from shot to shot, from groups of shots to groups of shots, that make a story a motion picture story and not a series of still photographs."

Putting yourself in the place of the home viewer makes you a better editor. In effect, the mind continually cuts from one picture to another in much the same way as well edited film does. For example, the much used sequence of long-medium-closeup shots makes sense when you think in terms of how you normally observe things. First you see the parking area, then your car, and finally the ticket on the windshield.

For smooth editing, one shot must lead to the next. Just as the mind and eye move from one "shot" to the next with a purpose, so should film. We go from medium to close in our view or attention because there's a reason we want to look closer. Meaningless closeups are a bore in film as in real life.

A cut is smooth when two shots go together without a jerk and continuity of action is not broken for the viewer.

A *jump cut* results from joining two discontinuous parts of a continuous action. Instantly, from one frame to the next, the speaker jumps from the left to the right side of the screen, or the hand held high comes down in 1/24 second. Such effects, too often seen as film cuts from voice-over to SOF of a speaker, defy reality and are visually annoying. A solution is to insert a cutaway shot of the audience between the discontinuous shots of the speaker.

Cutaways

In addition to covering jump cuts, cutaways can add perspective and show relationships. The cheering crowd, the disagreeing coach or the scoreboard (a highly utilitarian cutaway) are actually part of the story of a basketball game. And shots of children reacting are as important as those of fireworks, clowns or Santa Claus. Action brings reaction. A team scores—the crowd cheers. The band marches—the child watches.

Use only appropriate cutaways. Don't put a shot of smiling spectators between two serious SOF segments from a speech. One problem in shooting cutaways in advance of an event rather than in natural order is that they can easily look slightly out of place to the perceptive viewer.

Cutaways can compress time. Parts of a four-hour event may be shown in a 45-second newsfilm story and yet maintain continuity. Cutaways between one piece of action and the next help bridge time gaps. From a roaring fire, we cut to a closeup of the chief talking into a radiophone mike, and then cut back to the fire, which is now under control. Incidentally, a cutaway of spectators would not be appropriate there because they are looking at the fire and the impression would be "what a change they saw take place in those three seconds!"

Avoid intercutting steady and slightly shaky shots—the kind of contrast often found between tripod-braced and hand-held camera work. Continuity suffers when you cut from a steady main shot of the speaker to a shaky cutaway of the crowd and then back to the steady speaker.

Closeups

An editor's life is easier when there are plenty of closeups. They are the most versatile of shots. An editor can go to or from a closeup to just about any other shot, including most other closeups. By contrast, going to and from long and medium shots of subjects like buildings can bring visual jumps and jolts.

TV is a closeup medium. The home screen seldom exceeds 27

inches diagonally, and detail tends to be lost in long shots which would be impressive on a theatre's wide screen. The television closeup, on the other hand, shows people and their emotions as no other medium can.

Matching and Completing Actions

Consecutive shots of a single scene should match. If an angry man is shaking his fist at the end of one shot, he should be doing the same if his hand shows in the next shot. If the second shot is an extreme closeup of his head only, there's no problem. This is one reason the tight closeup can be so useful in editing. Less is shown which can contribute to discontinuity of action.

Matching two or more shots of a single movement such as the closing of a door is difficult, and even if achieved, is usually less effective than confining single movements to single shots. Though opinions differ on this, the authors have found that it is easier to cut between rather than within movements such as a ribbon cutting or Christmas tree lighting. Try cutting from shot to shot at moments of rest in the action. The MS stops with the governor or president ready to act. Then, the CU shows the action of snipping the ribbon or throwing the switch.

Avoid cutting out in the middle of action the viewer expects to see completed—such as a door closing, a tree falling or a truck dumping. In some cases a brief cutaway ai.d return to the main action to compress time (as in the case of a slow truck dumping) may be appropriate.

Getting into or out of a shot in the middle of movement such as a pan, zoom or dolly is often (though not always) jolting. Put yourself in the place of the spectator, since that is what the home viewer becomes. You normally like a moment to establish yourself before turning your head to survey (pan) a scene or moving your attention in (zoom or dolly) on a single aspect of it. If the shot ends before one of these movements is over, the viewers may be unhappy that they never quite got to wherever the film started taking them.

Screen Direction

As discussed in Chapter 3, violation of the logic of screen direction plays disconcerting tricks with reality. One moment the parade is moving from left to right on the screen and the next moment it's going from right to left. The sudden 180-degree shift in perspective is too much. If for some reason you want to change sides of the street, take the viewer with you gradually by using a headon shot of the parade for transition.

For two persons to face in opposite directions is visually consistent with their taking opposing sides on an issue. In the separate interviews with two political opponents, one might be looking slightly to the left of the screen and the other slightly to the right. This is especially recommended for intercut editing, where the film goes back and forth between brief statements by two persons. Not only does this scene composition parallel the two-sided audio content. It also helps the editor avoid the slight visual jumps which tend to result from joining identically composed shots, even when they are of different people or things.

Exposures

If film exposure is erratic, try to group the darker and lighter shots together as the story permits rather than going back and forth between dark and light. A very dark scene followed by a very light one, when projected on television, can produce an unpleasant transmission effect called "overshoot," which is the automatic equipment's reaction to a sudden light intensity change.

Similarly, avoid scenes in which a properly exposed face or other object is against a white or washed-out background, as would be the case in shooting your subject in front of a window. In adjusting to the lighter background, the automatic shader will tend to turn the foreground object into a silhouette.

Patterns

Any pattern—even the useful LS, MS, CU sequence—can become monotonous if over-used. So avoid becoming just an efficiently mechanical editor. Don't strain to be different or arty, but don't be afraid to try something a little different when it seems to help tell the story. Variation is part of the language of film.

BASIC SOUND-ON-FILM

Most of the principles of editing silent film also apply to sound-on-film. But the added dimension adds further considerations for the editor.

Natural Sound

Natural sound of a crowd, a parade or an airport can sound very unnatural. If sequences in which the shots look continuous do not also sound continuous, the listener-viewer will not feel like a witness to reality. Unfortunately, when time elapses between shots, continuity of sound is not as easily achieved as continuity of the visual. Thus natural SOF must be cut for the ear as well as the eye, though the judgment of the eye may have to take priority.

Natural sound tracks should be listened to carefully. The concern is not only for something offensive but for sounds which are simply distracting or confusing—the background conversation that ends in mid-sentence when the film is edited, the reporter's instructions, or the photographer's colorful comments. And what sounded natural on the scene may sound like a strange "whoosh" on television. If the desired sound does not reproduce adequately, the film may best be run as silent.

With natural SOF, shots should normally be allowed to run longer than with silent film. In most cases, good natural sound should make the film so much more interesting that shots can run longer without the viewer's feeling the need for visual change which tends to come with silent film.

Voice Sound

When SOF is of the spoken word, the sound track rather than the picture normally determines where cuts are made.

Editing voice SOF is complicated by the fact that the frame of picture and the sound which goes with it are not located side by side on the film. Instead, the sound is recorded and played back 28 frames ahead of the picture. The lens is near the top of a projector and the sound pickup near the bottom. As the film winds through from the top, just over one second of earlier picture precedes the start of a sound take. Conversely, at the end the picture runs out one second earlier than the sound.

As long as the speaker has a one-second pause before and after the sound cut, there is no problem. You can easily cut on sound at the start and on picture at the end.

However, if the needed pause before the first word is missing, the result can be *"lip flap."* The viewer sees up to a second of the speaker's lips moving without hearing what they say. About the only solutions are B-roll cover or use of an SOF transposer, to be discussed under "double system" later in this chapter.

Cutting immediately after the last word of a sound segment can give exactly the opposite problem—the viewer hears but does not see the final one second of the speaker. If the film ends with that SOF cut, the picture for the last one second of sound will be *blank screen* or reporter-on-camera, unless the editor has taken steps to cover the final one second of sound with appropriate picture.

Erasing the unwanted sound from the needed picture cover is one solution. A magnet lightly rubbed over the tape stripe on magnetic film will erase it, but be careful to protect the sound you *do* want. A good way to insure against erasing too far is to "under-wipe" the stripe— erasing a bit on the short side, checking the results, and then wiping a little more as needed. Many editors erase only as a last resort because a "pop" sound may accompany the return to magnetic SOF from erased film. Another solution is to cut on sound and splice on a "cover" shot of silent or natural sound film which is visually compatible with the preceding voice SOF cut. To avoid having a new picture come on for only a second or two, let such a cover shot run long enough to permit a closing of narration to be heard with it. "Covering" aside, such a wrapup often helps an SOF story achieve a fitting close-out.

The potential one second of sound without picture at the end of a shot may be covered by the lip flap at the start of an adjoining shot of the same person. But if you are splicing together such shots and there is no lip flap at the start of the second one, try to include those 28 frames of cover after the sound on the first shot. Some editors routinely cut when possible at the end of the speaker's natural pause at the end of the first shot, and they say the beginning of the second shot will usually take care of itself.

A cutaway on B-roll, to be discussed later, is often the best solution.

Lead-ins and Bridges

The story will usually look better if voice SOF cuts are surrounded by silent or natural SOF film rather than newscaster-on-camera. For example, a long silent or natural sound shot of the mayor's news conference sets the viewer up for the first voice SOF cut. Voice-over by the reporter runs back of the lead-in film. Similarly, film of the event or a reporter's standup usually provides a better visual bridge between voice SOF cuts than does returning to newscaster-on-camera.

Natural SOF generally does the job better than silent footage. Many SOF photographers regularly shoot natural sound for such shots as a crowd applauding, an attentive crowd when no one is speaking, a dignitary's car arriving, or airport activity. Such natural sound can enhance the film's reality as well as eliminate the "pop" which may come upon returning to SOF from silent film.

If silent film cutaways are put on B-roll, of course, there need be no interruption of SOF audio from the main ("A") roll of film.

"Back-up" lead-ins to SOF can be effective. If there is nothing vital in the few seconds of SOF preceding the cut you want, you can back up—say 10 seconds—and use that 10 seconds of video to cover the lead-in narration. The sound may be erased from this lead-in footage

or, preferably, the writer will cue it to be held under (low, as natural sound in the background), then brought up to full level 10 seconds in.

Some editors feel more secure against upcutting or missing the first word or two of a voice SOF cut if they precede it with a distinctly different shot. For example, 6 seconds of the station's reporter at the interview or news conference would suffice. If 6 seconds of intro words are placed back of this shot, the voice lead-in should hit the SOF precisely. Of course, if you "back up" 6 seconds and the film comes up as scheduled, this should be equally precise.

Air time can usually be saved by starting an SOF cut with an answer rather than the reporter's question. Answers often stand without questions. When they don't, paraphrasing in the story's narration may be more efficient than running the question. If two questions are being answered and the lead-in poses both, pose the question for the first answer just before hitting the SOF.

IN A FILM CHAIN, newsfilm images are projected into a TV camera for conversion into electronic signals for broadcasting. Jan Bieri threads a projector on a WHA-TV, Madison, Wis., film chain.

SOUND WITH B-ROLL

Separate reels of newsfilm can be rolled at the same time on two film chains, the projector-camera complexes which feed film into the station's TV signal. The director can then use any combination of the two sources of picture and two sources of sound. The separate reels are designated A-roll and B-roll. The A-roll usually includes the main SOF and the B-roll may be SOF or silent. Still other actuality sources, such as audio tape running on a cartridge chain, may be fed into the mix.

The example on page 125 indicates how these separate chains may be brought in and out and blended into a package. In this script by Karen Mawhinney for WTMJ-TV, Milwaukee, the story starts with B-roll picture over audio tape (CART 1-540) of Terry Heaton, whose voice is identified by superimposing his name over the bottom of the screen from a slide insert.

Twenty seconds in, we stay with B-roll picture (video) but go from Heaton tape cartridge to A-roll SOF for audio, which is from an interview with Tom Thiele.

Twelve seconds later, video is switched to A-roll and we see Thiele, as another slide is superimposed to tell us who he is.

At 50 seconds in, the picture dissolves back to B-roll while audio continues from A-roll.

At 1:14 in, it's back to A-roll to stay until the director takes the story off at 2:06.

With such precision timing, video cues describing the shots are not necessary. Indeed, for this kind of double-chaining, they would tend to clutter the page. But you can be sure that well-timed video appropriate to audio was mapped out precisely at the editing stage.

This *double-chaining* permits the director to do electronic fades, dissolves and superimpositions which are out of the question in the average film editing room.

B-roll scenes can also permit SOF on A-roll to run in longer takes, thus reducing the problem of audio jump cuts.

In its early use, B-roll was quite simple. If an SOF sequence contained a jump cut, for example, the cutaway was loaded on a second projector and rolled at the appropriate time to provide video to substitute for that surrounding the jump cut. Or actuality film would be rolled and shown from the second (B-roll) projector to illustrate points being made by the talking head on the main (A-roll) projector. The B projector would be started and stopped according to need.

Although this start-stop method is still in use, the more common

B-Roll Story Used on WTMJ-TV, Milwaukee

ELECTRIC CAR
KM
2 :20

ANNCR

Thirteen months ago, a group of men at the Allis Chalmers

Company put their heads together and built an electric car.

The strange car is owned by Tom Thiele (TEE-lee) of Oconomowoc.

Tom's put about 11-thousand miles on it so far -- just driving

it back and forth to work.

DOUBLE CHAIN FILM ------ SOUND ------ 2:06

SIMULTANEOUS ROLL

:00 B-ROLL SOUND UNDER
CART 1-540 FULL
SLIDE INSERT: HEATON -- OVER B-ROLL

:20 B-ROLL VIDEO CONTINUES
A-ROLL AUDIO FULL

:32 DISSOLVE TO A-ROLL: ON TIME
NAME INSERT: THIELE

:50 DISSOLVE TO B-ROLL: ON TIME

1:14 DISSOLVE TO A-ROLL· ON TIME

2:06 OUT ON TIME....ENDS ON NATURAL SOUND

approach now is to edit both the A-roll and B-roll to the same length and roll them simultaneously. Leader is edited into the gaps between film on the B-roll, and the A-roll if it has any gaps. Leave enough video overlap on both rolls to guard against momentary blank screen in switching from one projector to the other. The two rolls are timed simultaneously by running them through the interlock wheels of a multi-ganged (wheeled) synchronizer.

Ideally the A-roll and B-roll projectors are on separate film chains, allowing the director to easily "take" or "dissolve" in changing from one to the other. But if only one film chain is available, the B-roll film can be put on videotape, which can then be rolled in place of a film projector.

Insurance against on-air errors, especially when production is complex, can be provided by putting the final product on videotape in advance of the news program. Then at airtime the package is ready to go, requiring only one punching up of the videotape. Some stations have regularly scheduled late afternoon taping sessions for this purpose. But such taping is not always feasible.

Other B-roll pointers are included in a staff memo prepared by Tom Houghton, news director at WRC-TV, Washington, when he held the same position at WBZ-TV, Boston:

> Since we use the stopwatch system now—and since the essence of the stopwatch system is synchronized editing—the re-editing will cut everything utilizing more than one chain on a double-gang synchronizer . . . and, of course, will cut double-chain films to be rolled *simultaneously.*
>
> Houghton example:
>
> (DOUBLE CHAIN)
>
> (MAG SOF "A" WALLACE 1:00)
>
> KEY/VIDEOGRAPH: Wallace @ :00
>
> (TAKE "B" pix-only from :10 to :26)
>
> (TAKE "B" pix-only from :45 to :55)
>
> (ENDS. ". .why I will be president.")   (FAST OUT!)

Both chains roll at once. Director takes the Wallace sound-bite on the "A"-chain and covers two jump-cuts with "B"-chain silent. Director supers at the top . . . and, of course, the "fast out" indicates a minimal amount of film left after out-cue.

We always should shoot "cover" silent and reverse questions, but these are for editing protection and should not be used unless warranted. Don't use either just for the sake of using it. And, hereafter, do not use "A"-chain cutaways (i.e. 12 frames of silent sandwiched between two sound bites). Instead, use "B"-chain cutaways—even for brief "cover" occasions.

Narration and other sound-on-film (except background SOF) belong on the "A"-chain. Cover silent or background SOF ("natural" or "wild" sound) belongs on the "B"-chain.

EDITING DOUBLE-SYSTEM SOUND is best done with a special editing table such as this one at WHA-TV, Madison, Wis. The picture is on one reel and the synchronized sound on the other. This eliminates editing problems which result from the 28-frame gap between picture and sound on single-system SOF. The double-system sound reel consists of "fullcoat," 16mm perforated film base which is fully coated with a metallic oxide. Its surface looks essentially like that of audio tape.

DOUBLE-SYSTEM SOUND

Lip flap and other editing problems stemming from the 28-frame gap between audio and viedo on single-system film can be eliminated by the use of a *displacement recorder* and double-system editing equipment.

In the first phase of its operation, the displacement recorder "displaces" (erases and re-records) the sound track to put audio alongside video. In cutting on the word, you are also cutting on the right picture. When the film has been edited, the process is reversed, putting the film back into proper "sync" for projection, which means the sound is again 28 frames ahead of picture.

While double-system is still not used regularly for daily newsfilm work by many stations, a number of them use a hybrid type of SOF editing which combines double-system and A and B roll.

Under this approach, sound film is shot single-system and the rough editing is done single-system. At this point, editing is done to sound, not to picture. Then the sound track is transferred to sprocketed 16mm audio tape which is called "fullcoat" and is the audio part of double-system. The rest of the editing proceeds as in double-system.

The film and the audio track ("fullcoat") are placed in a 16mm synchronizer and both are given their final editing ("fine cutting").

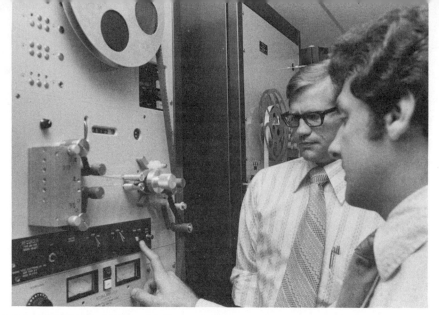

DOUBLE-SYSTEM SOUND MIXING is done at WRC-TV (NBC), Washington, in a special sound studio arrangement whereby up to five synchronized sound tracks can be mixed into one. Senior Film Editor John Long operates the console as News Director Tom Houghton calls the shots for a story. One source of sound can be a reporter's narration from the soundproof booth where the film is projected.

A DUBBER/RECORDER is at the heart of the WRC-TV editing operation.

Needless pauses can be removed from the audio track so long as the same length of film is also removed. Cutaways and other shots can be edited in to replace jump cuts or other visual bad spots. The audio track, having already been transferred, is irrelevant to this editing step. The 16mm film and the 16mm fullcoat are then played on the air on synchronized projectors.

The on-air result is similar to B-roll. It allows the editor to insert cutaways over jump cuts, replace talking-head video with film illustrating what is being talked about, and add visual variety to long takes of natural SOF. The editor has more flexibility in cutting film once the sound transfer has been made, and the director's job is far easier than when switching back and forth between film chains for A-roll and B-roll stories. To use this technique, the station must have special editing equipment and a machine interlocked to the projector to play the 16mm sprocketed fullcoat.

WRC-TV's system of double-system sound mixing is described by News Director Tom Houghton:

> We edit film "double-system": picture on one track, sound on the other(s). But, if you have several sound tracks (narration, effects, music, etc.), it takes extra interlocked sound and projection equipment and split-second switching to put it together on-the-air without having someone push the wrong button. So, we've installed a $30,000 sound studio to pre-mix up to five synchronized sound tracks into one.
>
> The components include 16mm recorders, dual reproducers (dubbers), a JAN projector, a footage counter, an Ampex ¼" recorder, a 5:1 mixing console, and a narration booth. There are similar units elsewhere, but experts from Magna-Tech, the manufacturer, claim the planning and layout make this the best news sound studio they've seen.
>
> The reporter in the booth narrates the edited film (projected on a screen) while the editor at the console funnels the narration and other sound sources into a single 16mm track.
>
> We use it on about 90% of our local stories and are servicing the station documentary unit and some network (NBC) units. We thought it would take more time than the old method, but it doesn't. In fact, the reporter is freed to pursue other assignments. Quality is guaranteed and the possibility of error is almost eliminated.

Unlike many other techniques treated in this book, double-system editing can be learned only by working with the equipment under the supervision of experts. Most of our brief treatment of the topic has been intended mainly for professionals who may gain by awareness of methods like WRC-TV's. Beginners need only be aware that such highly sophisticated methods of editing sound for film exist.

WITH AUDIO TAPE

The silent camera and the cassette tape recorder can make an effective team on some stories. Suppose that only silent film of a riot is available. The silent footage alone many be interesting but one-dimensional. Accompanying the film with sounds of the riot as picked up by the tape recorder makes the story come alive. When such independently taped sound is used back of silent film, it is called *wild sound.*

Wild sound can enhance such film as that of parades, windstorms, shopping and rush hour traffic. Caution: To be sure of true sounds, record them fresh each time. A sound-effects record of traffic sounds may have been recorded in New York City in 1954, and motor vehicles sound different now. Even today, the traffic sounds of New York are not necessarily those of Des Moines or Dallas.

Be sure it fits. A strange effect results from watching a drum solo while listening to a trumpet being featured with no drums audible.

Wild sound in the hands of a skillful editor or producer can come off well. Indeed, for an event like a parade, wild sound may work better than natural SOF if there's a lot of cutting from scene to scene. With wild sound, a single audio cut can run across several scenes and you avoid the annoyance of excessive audio changes which can come with natural SOF.

However, let it be emphasized that natural SOF is usually better. Too often, wild sound is just not quite the real thing.

Short audio tape segments of a speaker can occasionally be used to good effect behind silent film. Limit yourself to shots which do not give away the lack of lip sync—very long shots of the speaker, side shots, back shots, cutaways, anything but closeup or medium shots which will show that the speaker's lips and voice are not saying the same things. (Don't try to synchronize wild sound to a speaker's lips. The odds are against you.)

An example: You have a 20-second audio segment of a speech from the state senate and only silent film. Open with two or three shots including a closeup of the speaker, and use this film to cover the narrator's lead-in to the tape. While the tape is being heard, the film might be showing an LS cutaway of the legislature, LS wide from rear of chamber, CU cutaway of a listener, and an LS of chamber from back of the speaker.

As long as the tape excerpt is brief—say 30 seconds or less—this procedure can work. But used clumsily or too often, this substitute for voice SOF will look contrived to the discerning viewer.

A better use of audio tape over silent film is to use the sound of someone talking simultaneously with pictures of what the person is talking about. The mayor describes a traffic problem while we watch film of the problem. Or we hear the fire chief telling about the fire while we watch it burning. This technique is similar to double-chaining SOF.

EDITORIAL DECISIONS

The chief gatekeeper for taste and fair play in newsfilm is the editor. The photographer may well follow the rule of "if in doubt, shoot it," because a shot can always be edited out.

The editor may then have to decide what to do about shots of crying faces or mutilated bodies. Which should take priority—the public's curiosity or a person's desire for *privacy*?

What of the cute but *embarrassing* shot of a hard working legislator caught momentarily napping at his desk? It may draw a big laugh. But are you sure it is fair to the legislator?

What of other *unflattering* shots? Like a distorted profile of a governmental official you do not like? Try to resist the temptation.

What of those shouted *obscenities* on the film? They are part of reality. But are your viewers ready for this kind of reality?

Answers are not always easy.

One rule you can always follow is *never* to *deceive or mislead* the viewer. Let the edited newsfilm be as true as possible to the reality it is presented as reporting.

What of changing the order of SOF excerpts from a speech? If the newsiest one happened to come near the end, good journalism says move it up to the head of the film story. Actual order is usually irrelevant in such situations. But if *changing order* distorts content in any way, don't do it.

What of splicing together two SOF excerpts to *appear continuous* when in fact they were separated by a portion of the speech which is not being shown? Again, as long as the final product is true to what the speaker said and gives no false impression, go ahead.

But what of placing part of an answer to one question in such a position that it sounds like a response to a different question? Don't do it.

Are not *cutaways* often edited in rather than shot in the sequence shown? Yes, and they sometimes look it. Be careful that cutaways are consistent with adjoining shots in content. If they honestly represent the situation, the actual shooting sequence is irrelevant. But do not insert applause for a speaker who did not get it or show only bored audience cutaways for one who did. That's dishonest editing.

How about pulling some film from the files to illustrate today's story? After all, one city council meeting looks pretty much like another. Yes, but the practice remains deceptive unless you clearly label *"library film"* as such.

Should you use film *handouts*? Those often well produced films come from government, industry and other outside sources. Treat them with the same editorial judgment as any other incoming material. If a film handout contains newsworthy material, you may use that part. Otherwise, throw it out. If you use such outside film, clearly identify its source.

What if the Sales Department says a leading *sponsor* wants a newsfilm story done on a ribbon-cutting? Tell the Sales Department your newsfilm assignments are not for sale.

What if a governmental official asks for *outtakes*—film you did not use but happened to save? Before handing anything over, check your news director, who may in turn check station management and legal counsel. The request or subpoena should probably be fought. Like a reporter's notes, film outtakes are usually the business of no one outside the organization. Your giving in without a fight would set a bad precedent for those other editors who still believe the First Amendment applies to all news media.

Above all, let the answers to such questions come from you and your fellow broadcast journalists—not from outsiders.

REMINDERS

- Throw out soft, improperly exposed or shaky film. One bad shot can spoil the effect of an otherwise good story.
- Check film for bad splices or torn perforations before airing.
- Keep the splicer and editing table clean.
- Edit film so that one shot leads logically to the next.
- Include cutaways to avoid jump cuts, add perspective, show relationships and compress time.
- Group darker and lighter shots together as much as is practical to avoid "overshoot" effects in transmission.
- In editing voice SOF, let the sound track primarily determine where cuts are to be made.
- Lip flap can be covered by use of B-roll or double-system editing.
- Never distort the reality of an event or situation by editing simply to make a more "interesting story." Journalism takes precedence over show business.
- SOF cuts from a speech or interview may be rearranged as long as this does not distort what was really said.
- Do not use library film unless you label it as such.
- Do not use film handouts unless you identify the source.
- In general, resist outside requests for film outtakes.

8 | Writing for Newsfilm

Editing and scripting are best approached as a unitary process and done by the same person or a closely knit team. The survey conducted for this book showed that reporters do most of the writing for newsfilm at about half of the stations which have RTNDA news directors and share the job with other writers at another fourth of these stations. In about a third of the cases, the reporter is also the photographer. Only rarely is writing done by a photographer who is not also serving as reporter.

COORDINATION WITH EDITING

Union regulations prescribe separate editors and writers in some operations. Even then, editing should normally be done in terms of writing, and writing in terms of editing. In cutting film, the editor must be aware of the kinds of words needed to help tell the story. And the writer must use words appropriate to the scenes behind which they are to be read.

Audio-Video Fit

Sloppy fit between the narration and the scenes of newsfilm may be seen nightly on many stations and not infrequently on the networks. For example, a network correspondent's report on a California reception for a Soviet leader named celebrities present—Frank Sinatra, Art Link-letter and a couple of others. The celebrities were shown in the film but not at the points where their names were mentioned, their names were not superimposed when the celebrities did appear, and their appearances in the film were not even sequential with their mentions in the copy. Viewers who did not recognize the celebrities were left guessing.

A problem is word dominance, a tendency to use film largely to "illustrate" the words of a reporter. Too often a writer simply asks an editor for "50 seconds of the reception" with the assumption that any 50 seconds will do. The result tends to be poorly illustrated radio.

Good fit between film and copy is often made easier by the use of a *film-cut sheet* which lists shots or sequences and how long they run. About two-thirds of the respondents in the RTNDA newsfilm survey said their staffs often or usually worked from a slate of precisely timed shots or sequences.

Edit-Script or Script-Edit?

Which should come first—newsfilm editing or scripting? The answer can vary from story to story, and the best general rule is to give priority to the more important element of the particular story—the film or the reporter's words.

If the film is the primary communicator, editing should probably precede scripting. This is often the case for features, sports action, civil disorder, and accidents or disasters.

But if it's a "word" story, with film used largely to illustrate, then film should probably be cut to fit script. Examples: lead-ins or bridges for voice SOF, silent or natural sound film of meetings, or B-roll of buildings, traffic or wheat harvesting.

The survey conducted for this book showed that the cutting, or editing, of sound-on-film usually preceded its scripting at 55% of the stations. But scripting usually came first for silent film at 79% of the stations.

Many newsrooms take the approach of WDBO-TV, Orlando, Florida, described by News Director Ben Ayerigg: "Film is cut to match script to save time as deadline approaches. When film video commands, then script is written to match film."

A number of newsfilm supervisors said that, in a majority of cases, they would prefer cutting film first, but that it came out of the processor so late they had to write the copy while the film was still in the tanks in order to get it on the air. Adjustments must be made to such realities, of course, but only bad management permits such editing and scripting binds to become the rule rather than the exception. To hold all film for

a single processing run late in the day is false economy. At least two
or three runs spaced across the day are needed to give a staff time to
do justice to most newsfilm editing-scripting.

WRITING FOR SILENT FILM

Until experience has taught you how to abbreviate the procedure
without loss of precision, writing for silent film is best done from a
fully slated film-cut sheet. As each word is written, you are aware of
what will be on the screen when it is read. Example:

LS hiway wreck 5 sec.

LS knock down bridge 4

CU hiway crack 2

CU dump asphalt 3

MS dump asphalt 4

MS sweep road 3   TOTAL: 21 seconds

Develop a formula whereby a specified number of lines or words
of copy go with a specified number of seconds or feet of film. For example, 2 seconds of film may go with one 35-space line, or 5 seconds of
film with two 40-space lines. The formula working best for your newsroom depends on such factors as whether oversized type is used and
how fast your reporters read. The earthquake script example on page
137 uses 3 seconds of film for each 50-space lines. (This film produced
for the Automobile Manufacturers Association was distributed to TV
stations by National Television News, a producer of news and promotion
films.)

Note from the film-cut timing for the first sequence that all shots
are appropriate to the narration to be heard as they are seen.

Note also that video and audio cues are in ALL-CAPS, and copy to
be read is in regular case. This style is used by most stations.

Video cues should be brief and visually descriptive.

Don't write a separate bit of narration for each shot. That gets
choppy and artificial. Instead, look for logical groupings of shots and
write a block of copy for each such sequence.

Clear identification is made easier by starting a new block of copy
to accompany the establishing shot of whatever is to be identified. In
the earthquake film, this has been done for the Veterans Hospital and
Olive View Hospital.

Because there may be a slight pause in narration (reporter's voice
over) between blocks of copy, the last shot in a sequence is ideally one
which can carry itself without words if necessary. Sweeping the road,

National Television News

EARTHQUAKE CLEAN-UP CONTINUES IN LOS ANGELES

Most Los Angeles residents are back to near-normal today; but the long

earthquake clean-up job will take many months to complete.

(SCENES)   (SUGGESTED NARRATION)

LS HIGHWAY WRECKAGE   Buckled freeways and the collapse of a dozen
LS KNOCK DOWN BRIDGE
CU CRACK IN HIGHWAY   overpass bridges snarled traffic in San Fernando
CU DUMPING ASPHALT
MS DUMPING ASPHALT   Valley. In the city which depends on the motor
MS SWEEPING ROAD
   (21 seconds)   vehicle as its basic form of transportation, top

                          priority has been given to restoration of normal

                          driving conditions. Debris is being removed and

                          repairs are being made to roadways.

LS DUMPING RUBBLE   At the Veterans Hospital near Sylmar, where more
LS TRUCK W/PALM TREE
MS DUMP TRUCK   than 30 persons died, the search continues for more
CU ANDY GUMP
MS POWER TRUCK, PAN   victims as rubble is collected, dumped into trucks
  TO BARRIER TRUCK
   (31 seconds)   and taken away. Government agencies, business

                          and industry have pitched in to keep basic public

                          services operating during the clean-up. Most

                          broken gas and water lines have been restored.

                          More than one thousand persons were injured in the

                          quake; damage estimates vary, but the total loss

                          may well reach a billion dollars.

MS FIRE TRUCK, ZOOM   At Olive View Hospital three persons died, and the
  TO RUBBLE
LS HOSPITAL   23 million dollar structure was declared a total loss.
MS LOADING TRUCK
CU LOADING   Workmen know the clean-up job will be a long one,
   (14 seconds)
                          as Los Angeles recovers from its worst earthquake

                          in many years.

                (TOTAL RUNNING TIME: 66 SECONDS)

AUTOMOBILE MANUFACTURERS
ASSOCIATION

panning from truck to truck, and loading a truck are such shots. A pause back of any of these will not sound unnatural.

How much blocking and cueing you do depends on how much co-ordination is needed between copy and film. Some films, often the best, are self-explanatory throughout, and a single block of narration serves the whole story. And on a script for double-chained (B-roll) film, such detailed video cues would be omitted because they would tend to get in the way.

Blocking film copy too rigidly can stilt your style. Your thoughts and writing should flow from one block of copy to the next without artificial pauses which sound as if you are waiting for a cue. If you run over a bit on one block of copy, write the next one a bit short and it will balance out in most situations.

WRITING FOR SOUND FILM

The cut sheet for sound film must indicate its audio as well as video. The example on page 139, for a story reported by Henry Erb for WOTV, Grand Rapids, Mich., uses single-projection (A-roll only) and no silent film (only voice and natural SOF). The sound-under cue (S U) indicates that Erb will read copy while natural SOF is being projected, with the volume of the natural sound held down (under) enough that it does not interfere with his voice-over.

The story is told by natural SOF of a landfill and related scenes, voice SOF excerpts from interviews with Boerema and DeZwaan, and standup SOF of Erb used to open, close and bridge (after DeZwaan interview) the film package.

Cumulative timings are used within WOTV film sequences. Many stations time cumulatively from start to finish of a story.

Outcues (the last words said) for each voice SOF segment would normally be included, but Erb got into a time bind on this one.

In this case, the film-cut sheet was filled out and a script written before the film was physically cut (edited). But Erb had viewed the film carefully and edited it mentally, with the results going on the cut sheet.

KIRO-TV, Seattle, uses a similar film-cut sheet, and Managing Editor Clif Kirk explains how it works:

> Since reporters and cameramen work together on most stories in our operation, and then view the film together when it comes out of the processor, it is usually a simple matter to use these cut sheets, editing the film to fit the copy. In other words, the reporter has a pretty good

WOTV, Grand Rapids, Mich.

EDITING INSTRUCTIONS

						TOTAL
SLUG	**LANDFILL**	REPORTER	ERB	NEWSCAST	DATE	TIME 4:07

SIL/SU/SOF
TIME   ID's/OUTCUES/DP TIME

 SOF :10   ERB OPEN

 S U 1:14+1   :00   show County landfill   i d logo and fence

                                  :14   show some private haulers at county landfill

                                  :34   i d   waste management landfill (e belt)

                                  :42   show Industrial Disposal truck

                                        at w/m site

                                  :52   show public works board meeting

 SOF :19   BOEREMA INTERVIEW

 S U   :33+1   :00   show Boerema and Erb talking

                                  :16   i d   De Zwaan

 SOF :29   DE ZWAAN INTERVIEW

               ERB SOF BRIDGE

 S U   :48+1   :00   show landfill county site

                                  :16   g r trucks collecting

                                  :32   show waste management landfill site

 SOF :29+3   ERB STAND UP CLOSER

idea of what film is available and he is expected not to call for scenes which are not there. It is normally the reporter who fills out the cut sheet for the photographer/editor, though it can and sometimes does work the other way around, with the cameraman cutting the film for optimum visual effectiveness and giving the reporter a cut sheet showing how the film WAS edited. The reporter can then write his copy to fit the film.

Note that the KIRO-TV approach is flexible on whether writing or film cutting comes first. Either way, a precision rather than hit-or-miss or trial-and-error method is used. Once mastered, precision timing is faster and easier as well as more effective. The trial-and-error reporter or writer sits with a stop watch and projector and tries various wordings with the film until eventually something comes out about right. Such a time waster has no place in a busy newsroom.

In most use of B-roll, cumulative timing must be indicated on the script. An example of such double-chain film script is included in Chapter 7. Though stations use varying copy formats, the procedures noted in the following guide will do the job.

CLIF KIRK'S KIRO-TV WRITING GUIDE

LIVE: Sound on film may be used very much the same as silent film -- but with the added element of natural sound.

FILM /SOUND UNDER (:22)   If that's what you are doing, this is the way to show it. Please note that we have indicated here -- just as we did with the silent film -- exactly how much film there is for the anchorman to read over.

                                        For the purposes of _this_ example, though, the timing is even more critical. Because we are leading into a sound on film statement by Senator Throckmorton P. Foggybottom:

FILM/SOUND UP FULL: SOF at :22 - ENDS: "...WITH MY LAST BREATH."
MATTE: SEN. FOGGYBOTTOM (AT :30)
    TFT: 1:06

LIVE: Since the readover was 22 seconds, we showed
                                       <u>SOF at :22</u>. The senator talked for 44 seconds.
                                       That's shown by the <u>total</u> film time (TFT: 1:06)
                                       on the left at the point the film ends.

<u>DOUBLE CHAIN</u>
CHROMA STILL FRAME: Now, let's try a somewhat fancier and more
    (SENATE FLOOR)   "in-depth" report of the same story. This is a
                                       full "standup" report by Scoop Jones -- with
                                       audio carts and everything -- even a chroma still
                                       frame of the senate floor for the anchorman's
                                       lead-in.

FILM/SOUND UNDER/CART   <u>CART #16... :00 -- ENDS: "HOODWINKING THE PUBLIC."</u>
MATTE: JONES REPORTING

FILM/SOUND UP FULL: <u>SOF AT...:22 -- ENDS: "...WITH MY LAST BREATH."</u>
MATTE: SEN. FOGGYBOTTOM (AT :25)

FILM/SIL/CART   <u>CART #16 AT... 1:15 -- ENDS: "...FIST ON THE TABLE"</u>

FILM/SOF   <u>SOF AT... 1:27 -- ENDS: "...INCORRIGIBLE SCOUNDREL"</u>
MATTE: SEN. ROUNDHOUSE (AT 1:30)

"B" REEL...IN -- 1:35
          OUT -- 1:44

FILM/SIL/CART: <u>CART #16 AT... 1:52 -- ENDS: "...BAREKNUCKLE BRAWL"</u>

FILM/SOF: <u>SOF AT... 2:00 -- ENDS: (STANDARD CLOSE)</u>

         TFT: 2:22

LIVE: Note that right under the story slug we
                                       write "<u>DOUBLE CHAIN</u>" -- warning the director
                                       there are both "A" and "B" reels in this story.
                                           Second -- we are careful to put down
                                       EVERYTHING IN SEQUENCE -- whether it be film,
                                       mattes, "B" reel or whatever.
                                           Most important -- ALL TIMINGS ARE FROM THE
                                       BEGINNING OF THE FILM -- WHETHER SILENT OR SOF.
                                       The timings indicate when each segment <u>STARTS</u> --
                                       NOT HOW LONG IT IS. Total film time is given
                                       at the end of the film sequence.

Superimpose liberally. Names and identifications of people and places lettered across the bottom of the screen give the viewer information efficiently. They cut down on the amount of copy which must be used for IDs. Supers must be called for as video cues on the copy. An example of a story using many supers is provided in a portion of the copy for KTRK-TV film of storm damage in the Houston area.

Excerpt from KTRK-TV (Houston) Storm Film Copy

ROLL NAT SOF & CTR   TIME :35   ...Some 12-thousand phones in three exchanges

SUPER: LARRY CONNERS REPORTING   were out, but most had been restored by

                                        midnight. Police and firemen provided what

                                        assistance they could during the night.

ROLL SOF   TIME 1:05   C.C. "...till it was all over."

SUPER: LARRY CONNERS REPORTING

      EPSOM THEATRE
      9716 JENSEN

      ELMO WARD
      MOVIE PROJECTIONIST

      LARRY CONNERS REPORTING

      BELLMEAD AREA

      MRS. E.A. NEAL
      9913 ALDINE-WESTFIELD   TAKE B ROLL AFTER 10 SECONDS
                                          FOR 15 SECONDS.
      J.W. LEBOUEF
      EMERALD FOREST PARK

ROLL NAT SOF & CTR   TIME :30   The most visible damage occurred with the

                                        mobile homes. They were blown over, ripped

SUPER: CYPRESS-BELLMEAD AREA   apart, blasted to pieces...destroyed...even

                                        some which had been tied down. And yet

                                        nearby other mobile homes and dwellings were

                                        untouched. There are reports of injuries

                                        but none confirmed as serious. The rain,

                                        hail and wind damage does not yet have a

SUPER: LARRY CONNERS REPORTING   dollar value, but it will be substantial.

                                        Larry Conners, Eyewitness News.

WRITING STYLE

A leading consultant has called it part of "humanizing" the news. Others have called it writing "talk copy." Good writing for television is telling the story as one person to another, simply and directly with the words of everyday conversation. Save your convoluted sentences and erudite words for term papers. They have no place in the copy that goes with newsfilm.

Interpersonal communication is usually more effective than what we get from the mass media. If a friend tells you of something that happened downtown today, you're more likely to get the message than if your source is a newspaper or television story. One reason is that your friend will probably tell it in meaningful person-to-person terms, a form of expression used too little by newspaper and television news writers. Words to go with newsfilm should be written as if you were talking to another person, which is what happens when the copy is read on the air.

Direct Expression

Use a direct style of sentence construction—who-said-what, who-did-what, what-happened. Avoid backing in with such constructions as what-was-said-by-whom. Active verbs are usually better than passive.

Dangling attribution is not only unnatural for most talk copy, but it can make an opinion sound too much like that of the reporter rather than the source. Don't write: "Some of the environmentalists are nuts, the governor says." Make it: "The Governor says some of the environmentalists are nuts."

The indicative, when appropriate, is stronger than the subjunctive for future tense. Example: "The governor said he will (NOT "that he would") not run again."

Clauses tend to be more direct than verb-form phrases. Awkward: "Weekend reports of Donaldson's having suffered a stroke . . ." Better: "Weekend reports that Donaldson had suffered a stroke . . ."

Because small mouthfuls are easier to handle, a prepositional phrase after a word often makes a better modifier than an adjective preceding it. "Members of the United Nations" is easier to say than "United Nations members."

Identification

Identification is usually better used before than after a name. Example: "A Janesville attorney—William Hardin—announced today . . ." Especially if the identification is cued to the start of a film scene, this gives a couple of seconds leeway in case the scene is slow in coming up. If Hardin is to be shown, he should be on the screen when his name comes up, either in the narration or on a super.

Be especially careful with names and identifications in stories involving accidents or crimes. Ray Miller, KPRC-TV, Houston, has advised his staff:

> Be sure you get it right. Do not use tentative identification. And do not take the word of people at the scene that victims are dead. People, including police officers, often believe that injured people removed from a bad accident scene surely are dead. But they are often wrong. Do not report a death until a medical examiner has confirmed it at the scene, or a hospital has told you that the injured party was dead on arrival.
>
> Never identify individuals as robbers, rapists or murderers. You can say that a robber got 10-thousand dollars from the bank and that Joe Doakes was arrested a block away and charged with armed robbery. But you cannot say that Joe Doakes held up the bank or is a robber.
>
> Our suspects make "statements," never "confessions."

Avoid the Trite

Miller also tries to steer his writers away from some of the trite expressions heard too often in television news.

> "Shower activity" is always being referred to by the Weather Service and weathercasters. It means rain. And it has exactly the same standing in usage that "sunshine activity" would have. When you mean rain, say rain.
>
> Direct quotations usually add nothing unless you have the voice of the source and then you do not need to say the awkward "quote" and "unquote." It is also bad form to over-qualify quotes. When you say that the President says the Vice President is a genius, it is not necessary to say that "the President said the Vice President is, in his words, a genius." It is perfectly plain who said it.
>
> One of the most popular instances of bad usage today is "hopefully," employed to mean "it is hoped." Hopefully is a perfectly good word. One can pray hopefully, or look hopefully toward the east. But sentences like "This will happen tomorrow, hopefully" are hopelessly bad form and unworthy of you.
>
> It is also fashionable to have people "undergoing" operations or examinations. This is strained and contrived. If someone has an operation, say he had an operation, or had surgery. He does not have to "undergo" an operation every time.

No False Claims

> Some broadcast news organizations try to dress up their product with fake claims of exclusivity. Channel 2 News is not one of those organizations. Give our staff all the credit you reasonably can, without

making any false claims. KPRC-TV has no reporters regularly stationed in London and claims none. We do have newsmen all over Houston and, when it actually happens that way, you should make it a point to say that "_____ told Channel 2 News," etc.

"Said" Is a Good Word

Don't strain for synonyms for "said" or "says." Words like "stated," "declared" and "announced" should be reserved for the few specialized situations which they accurately describe. The best word is the one you would normally use in person-to-person talk, and that is usually "said" or "says."

Never use "noted" or "pointed out" for opinion statements. They imply an established fact which is there to be noted or pointed to. Example: "He said (NOT noted) that the big oil companies are to blame."

Don't Bog Down

You'll miss most listener-viewers if you cram too many different bits of information into the narration. Research has shown that people tend to watch news as they do entertainment—in a fairly relaxed manner. Try overworking their attention level and you're wasting your time. So use the narration to make a few points effectively rather than trying to nutshell every point available.

Round off large numbers when the exact figure is not essential. Who's going to remember the exact amount anyway? Unless there's some special reason for using 54,136, round it off to 54-thousand or "about 54-thousand." If the exact figure is really important, then superimpose 54,136 for best results.

Avoid unnecessarily cumbersome words. As examples, simplicity recommends "about" over "approximately," "begin" over "commence," "try" over "endeavor," and "buy" over "purchase."

And, of course, keep most sentences short.

Think

Do not use such time redundancies as "8 p.m. tonight" or "tomorrow morning at 7 a.m." It's "tonight at 8 o'clock," "tomorrow morning at 7," or "tomorrow at 7 a.m."

Television is a medium—not a media (plural).

Don't Over-Write

Good film can stand on its own to a great extent, especially if it has natural sound. So don't ruin its impact with too many words. The viewer is seeing the same thing you are, and does not need to be told that the plane is flying, the man is walking, or the ball went through the net. Former radio writers tend to belabor the obvious because they are accustomed to helping listeners visualize scenes through a non-visual medium. Radio play-by-play sportscasters are notorious for talking too much when doing a TV game.

A reporter coming from a rapid-fire radio format may try to crowd too many words into a minute. These cavalry-charge reports tend to be lost behind film, because primary attention in TV tends to go to the visual. It's self-defeating to overload the viewer with too much information per minute.

When there's natural sound and the film will carry itself, don't be afraid to pause. Some of the most effective newsfilm voice-over is that of Charles Kuralt of CBS-TV in his "On the Road" features. He never seems in a hurry, and he knows when to be quiet for a moment to let you sense the reality, for example, of an old train coming in or a swamp in repose.

But don't allow for a pause if the video at that point is too dull to carry itself. Silent film of meetings and other visual losers require full narration to keep the viewer awake. Furthermore, much of a pause back of a closeup of someone talking may falsely lead the viewer to think a sound cut is coming up.

Don't overwrite the final sequence, lest the film come out before the narration. Some stations like for the final scene to trail on for 3-4 seconds longer than scripted, as insurance against coming out early. Avoid putting vital action, such as the winning goal in a basketball game, in the last frames of a film story. There's too much risk that the director may cut out of the film a moment too soon.

Film and its copy should complement each other at every point. A station content to achieve this only most of the time is only almost professional—not quite.

REMINDERS

- Make sure that the narration is appropriate to the picture on the screen throughout the story. Using a film-cut sheet helps.
- When film is the primary communicator of the story, film-cutting should normally precede scripting.
- When film is used primarily to illustrate a "words" story, scripting should normally precede the film-editing.
- Use a formula whereby a specified number of lines or words of copy go with a specified amount of film.
- Use supers of IDs liberally.
- Identifications in the script are usually better placed before than after a name.
- Write person-to-person "talk" copy.
- Use direct, uncomplicated sentences.
- Be precise and accurate.
- Avoid trite expressions.
- Don't strain for synonyms for "said" or "says."
- Don't overload the script with detail.

9 | Film Processing

Shooting the newsfilm story of the year will be wasted effort if your award-worthy film dies in the processor. Such misfortunes befall everyone, but many of them can be prevented.

Although practices vary from station to station, many operations require that camera reporters occasionally do their own processing. The survey conducted for this book showed photographers or reporters operating film processors quite often at a third of the stations and now and then at many others.

To be in charge of processor maintenance or even to run one regularly, you should have far more technical knowledge than is provided here. This chapter is intended only as a basic orientation for the person who may be called upon to run the processor but who is not a lab technician.

Time and Temperature

In any photographic process, development of the image on film is a chemical reaction, therefore a function of time and temperature. This is important because in most processing systems it is the only measure of control an operator has over an otherwise highly automated process. It is easier to grasp the implications of time and temperature by a study of results than by theory. In reversal processing (development which yields a positive image on the film, used by most TV stations) the longer the film remains in the *first* developer and/or the higher the tempera-

148

A FILM PROCESSOR requires careful maintenance for consistently high quality film. WITI-TV, Milwaukee, Lab Technician John Koerner checks the crucial first developer, in which the film's basic image is determined, in negative form. It is then chemically "reversed" and re-developed in the next tanks to bring about the "reversal" process which enables the film to come out of the processor with a positive image. As the film continues through the processor, it is "fixed," washed and dried. The film magazine is loaded just to the left of the first developer, and the processed film comes out on the big reel beside the pipe at the same end of the processor. Tanks holding chemicals for replenishing are mounted above and to the rear.

ture of that developing chemical solution, the stronger (more developed) the image will be. The converse is true for a shorter time/lower temperature.

Let's accept at the outset that this is an oversimplification. Any variation from the recommended time/temperature ratio for a given film produces some other effects: graininess, increased or decreased contrast, loss of detail in highlights or shadows, possibly a shift in the tone of colors. Variations in time and temperature are also limited by the operating range of the processor and the physical characteristics of the film.

With most films in common use, the limits of exposure (development) control permit you to "force" film (produce a brighter positive image on it) about 3 f/stops or to "hold back" (underdevelop film which has been overexposed) by about 1 f/stop. Except in really special cases, avoid trying to force film more than 2 stops. The temperature boost necessary for a 3rd stop is such that it may take several hours for the solution to get back to normal for regular processing.

Given the inherent risks in altering the normal processing cycle, forcing or holding back should be thought of only as a last resort, a step to correct an error in original exposure or to compensate for lighting conditions which were inadequate and uncontrollable. To the photographic purist, something is always lost by varying from the normal. But in TV, news values must sometimes override technical standards.

Keep all processing solutions replenished as prescribed for the particular machine. Proper use of replenishers keeps the working solutions fully active, makes them last longer and saves mixing time. Most important, colors will come through better.

Labeling

Film destined for processing must always be labeled. In the case of daylight reels (usually 100 or 200 feet), the necessary information is best put on the reel itself in grease pencil. The information can be wiped off and the reel re-used. In the case of magazines (usually 400 feet or larger), the information should be written on paper or masking tape and attached to the reel. In any event, there must be some way to relate this information and any specific processing instructions to a specific piece of film. In a crowded lab, it is all too easy to mix up reels and do the wrong thing to a roll of film.

What sort of information? As a minimum, you need a "story slug" to identify the story and permit rapid sorting to get it back to the right reporter, writer or editor. Footage should be noted, as it tells the processor operator whether the amount of film to be run will fit in one magazine or require a second. The exposure information must be clearly marked by a system generally agreed upon by all photographers and lab technicians at the station. While the exposure can be given in terms of ASA ratings, it is easier to give special processing instructions in terms of f/stops—as "hold back 1 stop" or "force 2 stops." Any film requiring special processing must be separated from all which will run normally, and this must be indicated to the person in charge. If possible, film to be forced or underdeveloped should be put through the processor in a separate run.

"Going Dark"

Some checking before the lights go out in the loading room will prevent, at the very least, lost time and annoyance and, at worst, total disaster. It is good practice to turn on the processor, except for the drive mechanism, a half-hour before film processing begins. On most machines, there are electric heating units to control developer and drying temperature, and air or mechanical devices to recirculate solutions. While the film is being loaded, the processor can get up to proper heat, the chemicals can be recirculated to assure uniformity, and no time is lost after the film is loaded.

In the loading room itself, strict adherence to routine is essential. Once you have started, there is no turning on a light to find that missing stapler, the core that rolled away, the magazine lid or anything else. Lay out all necessary items in a standard pattern and learn by practice where everything is. Check the stapler—running out of staples can occur at awkward times. Count and lay out enough cores or reels to handle the load of film. Make sure there are scissors to cut leader or film. Leader is tough to tear by hand, and film collects far too many finger marks as it is.

As you prepare to load the film, inspect what you can see of it on the spool for any torn sprockets. A film tear can give way inside the processor, ruining part of the film and delaying the rest. The delay while the processor is being re-threaded can be a matter of hours if the machine is not stopped very quickly when the film breaks apart.

Loading Order

The steps in loading film vary somewhat according to the particular machine, but the following apply to most.

The order in which you put film onto the core or reel in the processor magazine is important and must be determined before the light goes out. In any event, the last film loaded will be the first off the machine. This can be critically important at deadline time. Perhaps as important is the handling of any film which requires special processing. It must be separated from other film by enough leader to permit the processor speed and temperature to adjust from the requirements of one film to the next before the film goes into that crucial first developer.

If there are doubts about which processor settings to use and time permits, a "test strip" of film can be run. If there is a 10-15 foot segment at one end of the reel (preferably the tail) which is not essential to the story, this can be clipped off, loaded and separated from the rest of the film by leader. If the leader is long enough, the test film can be visually inspected after it clears the stop bath. Adjustments in speed or temperature can then be made for better development of the body of the film.

Loading Precautions

Some common processing headaches can be prevented by attention to a few details in loading the film. In stapling film to leader or another piece of film, keep the edges in a smooth, *straight* line. A slight angle can cause difficulty in tracking over rollers, causing strain or even tear-ing the splice. Film or leader should overlap enough in a splice to be reasonably flexible. A short, stiff splice tends to hang up or put unnecessary strain on the film. Edges should be clean-cut, and staples should hold down each end of a splice. Loose ends can easily snag.

Do not rush through the loading. The extra few seconds it takes to *slowly* wind film onto the magazine core or reel are worth it. Rapid winding and abrupt stops can generate enough static electricity to expose film when it sparks. You may have seen film shot outdoors on a sunny day that included flashes of lightning. Other things can cause it, but the chances are good there was a spark in the loading room.

Finally, be sure to load the film in such a way that the backing side rather than the emulsion side will be in contact with the rollers in the processor. Emulsion is highly sensitive to abrasion at this stage when it is warm and wet, and it will most likely be damaged by scraping over rollers.

Before You Press "ON"

Give the processor a quick final inspection. Check the circulation in all tanks holding solutions which require agitation. Inadequate agitation can cause uneven development and streaking. Be sure that all lights or heating elements in the drying compartment are on. Film that is not completely dry (either because of heating element failure or excessive machine speed) can stick on the takeup reel, and there goes the ball game. Inspect the splices in the leader already in the machine. Ideally, splices should not be left immersed in chemicals for any length of time, but a close watch will detect deterioration before a costly break during processing.

General Considerations

Of course, everything can still do down the drain (literally) unless the machine is watched during operation. Once the film is committed to the processor, the slightest malfunction can destroy the whole run . . . *unless* someone is there to take corrective action. A break in a splice can sometimes be repaired in seconds . . . if someone is there to do it.

Cleanliness counts. A wise news director would ban smoking and eating in the vicinity of the machine and certainly in the loading room. Contamination of chemicals is surprisingly easy, especially in machines that use small quantities of chemicals.

Some chemicals used in film processing are highly toxic and may be lethal. It is dangerous to inhale the fumes over a prolonged period. Good ventilation in the film processing room is essential. Federal regulations may also require a shower nearby in the case of certain chemicals which produce serious burns when they come in contact with the skin.

Maintenance of most machines requires knowledge beyond that normally expected of a reporter or photographer. But preventive maintenance is largely a matter of cleanliness and record-keeping to anticipate trouble. Adequate logs help assure freshness and strength of chemicals, machine lubrication and other operational considerations. Such logs also provide a record of film usage (no small consideration for budget-conscious news directors) and a form of cost accounting to gladden the heart of any station controller.

Not every photographer will run a processor, but many will . . . and perhaps should, since it is still another important link in the process of communicating reality via television news.

REMINDERS

- Turn the processor on for heating and recirculation of chemicals before processing begins, ideally a half-hour in advance.
- Make sure the processor is set for the proper running speed and temperature, and that all processing solutions are in good condition.
- Check film for any torn sprockets or other weaknesses which might cause it to break during processing.
- Staple the ends of film or leader together carefully in a smooth, straight line with enough overlap for flexible movement over the processor's rollers.
- If time is critical, load the most important film onto the processing reel last, since that will make it the first out of the machine.
- Wind film on the processing reel slowly to avoid sparks from static electricity.
- Keep the processing area clean, neat and free of smokers.
- Never leave a processor unattended during a film run.
- If the film or leader breaks during a run, stop the machine immediately. The less distance between the two ends, the less rethreading will be necessary, the sooner you'll be able to staple the ends back together, and the less the film loss.

10 | New Tools for Camera Reporting

Now that you have learned to use 16mm newsfilm cameras, will they be replaced by portable electronic cameras? Or super 8? Or both? Or neither? As this was being written, answers to those questions remained varied and tentative.

Portable electronic cameras which use live transmission or videotape instead of film were showing great promise for television actuality reporting. Sophisticated new equipment was being developed, more stations were putting it into use, and others were waiting for the right equipment at the right price. Our 1973 survey showed only 3% of the RTNDA-represented stations making much use of the Minicam and its relatives, with 10% reporting a "little" use. But respondents at half of the stations said they expected the future to include electronic cameras for field reporting in their operations. At KPLR-TV, St. Louis, one of the first stations to move totally to portable videotape, News Director Bill Addison said, "It's just around the corner."

Super 8 film, long heralded as coming soon for television news, was being used regularly by about a dozen stations at the start of 1974. Ten per cent of the RTNDA survey respondents said they foresaw its use at their stations, and 11% were undecided. Several indicated they would like to switch from 16mm to the less expensive super 8 if it met their technical standards.

In any case, most of the basic techniques learned from 16mm newsfilm should carry over if you have occasion to use portable electronic cameras or super 8.

154

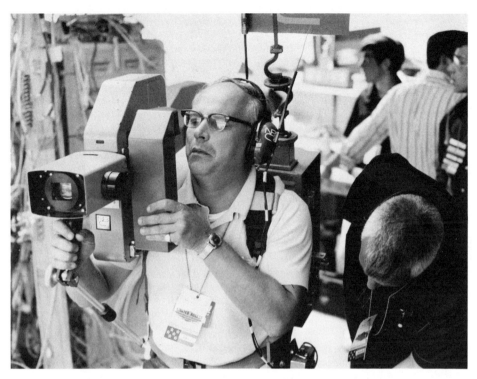

PORTABLE ELECTRONIC CAMERAS have been widely used by the networks in their coverage of such special events as political conventions. The picture and sound can be put on the air directly or recorded on videotape.

PORTABLE ELECTRONIC CAMERAS

No longer does live or videotaped news coverage require book-mobile-sized vans filled with equipment. The old disadvantages of electronic cameras—bulkiness and lack of portability—have been alleviated in miniaturized equipment.

A pioneer among the portable cameras was the PCP-90, developed by CBS Laboratories and produced by Norelco (Philips Broadcast Equipment Corp.). CBS dubbed it the Minicam. The networks and a number of their owned-and-operated stations began using this camera regularly for news coverage in 1972.

How They Work

The Minicam's 18½ pound camera head can easily be carried on the shoulder or mounted on a tripod. The only other essential piece of portable gear, the back-pack, weighs 12 pounds without battery, 32

VIDEOTAPE EDITING at most stations involves the simultaneous running of two videotape machines to dub the desired excerpts from one tape to another. Ed Furstenberg edits with the standard 2-inch tape machines at WHA-TV, Madison.

pounds with. An optional 100-foot cable to connect the camera head with the back-pack enables you to shed the back-pack as long as you stay within 100 feet of it.

The camera can be operated in three modes:

1) It can *record* on the scene, using a 2-inch reel-to-reel quadraplex videotape recorder, or a slant track tape recorder which is used with a time-base corrector for improved quality.

2) With a *microwave* package attached to the back-pack, it can transmit directly to a receiver, usually mounted on a high building, for relay to the station for live telecasting or for recording.

3) It can attach directly to a *video line*, again making it capable of live transmission or off-the-scene recording.

In addition to the PCP-90 (Minicam), increased use was being made of a smaller portable camera, a 12-pound unit developed co-operatively by CBS-TV and the Ikegami Tsushinki Co. of Japan. When connected with a 1-inch helical-scan cartridge videotape machine and a time-base corrector (to correct any picture instability), this camera produces air-quality pictures from a system costing considerably less than early models of the PCP-90.

Regardless of the camera used, the basic shooting techniques are much the same, and most of them utilize skills needed to shoot SOF. The camera must be steady, cutaways are needed, and the usual rules of composition and story-telling apply. Focus and exposure are critical.

Why Use Them?

A major advantage of electronic cameras is the speed with which they enable stories to be aired. As opposed to film—which must be taken to the station, processed, edited and projected—electronic equipment can put stories on the air live. Or tape can be put on without the time-consuming processing step necessary for film.

An electronic camera gives instant feedback from the viewfinder, eliminating unpleasant surprises such as soft focus showing up for the first time as film comes out of a processor.

Electronic cameras can operate at low light levels, and the use of existing room light means less camera crew obtrusiveness.

Few stations have facilities to copy a 16mm film for a second print. But making dubs from videotape is simple and quick, seldom taking more than two interconnected machines.

When airing videotape, the director generally has more technical options available than when airing film. For example, slow motion or freeze-frame can be easier with videotape.

Once the equipment has been purchased, electronic systems generally cost less to operate than 16mm SOF systems. Videotape can be reused (dubs can be made of on-air packages for the tape library). There are no chemicals to replenish and no processors to be concerned with.

Editing

One of the main reasons many stations delayed adopting portable electronic camera reporting was the difficulty of editing videotape fast and efficiently without editing equipment which was beyond the budget of the stations.

Without the special editing equipment, videotape editing requires two tape machines—one to play the original tape and the second to record the edited version. When an "edit" point has been located on the original tape, both tapes are rewound 7-10 seconds, then started at the same time. After the 7-10 seconds have passed and both machines are up to speed, a switch to record mode transfers the desired material to the new tape. Either audio or video, or both, can be edited in this way. It's a precision task which takes more time than physically splicing film.

With special computerized editing machines, videotape editing can be fast and efficient. The problem as this was written was that these machines were too expensive for most stations. But improving technology indicated machines for the future which would do the job and sell at a price the average station could afford.

In Use

The earliest use of portable electronic cameras was for news and sports coverage by the networks. They soon became standard equipment for political conventions. These roving cameras were also used at World Series baseball games, transmitting via microwave from anywhere in the stadium to a dish atop the scoreboard. From there the signal was fed to a remote van and on the air.

KTLA-TV, Los Angeles, installed a PCP-90 on its news helicopter. With remote controls and a microwave transmitter, the station was then able to provide live coverage of nearly any news event or disaster in the area—from a freeway accident to a forest fire. This also meant that KTLA-TV crews no longer had to fight Los Angeles freeway traffic.

For the most part, however, early network and station use of portable electronic cameras was for late-breaking stories and live productions such as political conventions. NBC started assigning its Washington crew for the afternoon and early evening, to be available for late-breaking news beyond the film processor's deadline. And, depending on the time available before going on the air, the story could either be recorded at the scene with the tape delivered to the station by motor-courier, or special arrangements could be made for microwave, or video line connections to feed the signal directly to the station.

The trend to miniaturization and portability of electronic cameras appeared certain to continue. By 1974, Magnavox was delivering a 7-pound color camera called the Chromavue 400 for about $2,500 which KDUB-TV, Dubuque, was claiming produced an air-worthy picture. The camera included a built-in microphone, a 4:1 f/2.5 zoom lens, and an automatic light range circuit. Fairchild, at the same time, was announcing a 6-ounce black-and-white television camera which was roughly the size of a package of cigarettes.

SUPER 8

The main attractions of super 8 over 16mm film are: 1) the greater portability of super 8 equipment, and 2) lower cost of operation. The main barrier to its use in television news has been its inability to produce quality comparable to 16mm film.

Easier Camera Reporting

Super 8 cameras are smaller and easier to operate than most 16mm models. The typical super 8 camera is less than half the size and weight of most 16mm counterparts. Film loading is nearly instant and foolproof with cartridges. No more fumbling around with loops and perf engagements. And practically all super 8 cameras have automatic

SUPER 8 FILM CAMERAS are usually more compact than comparable 16mm newsfilm cameras. This Wilcam sound-on-film camera used by KDUB-TV, Dubuque, Iowa, is a modified Minolta D-10.

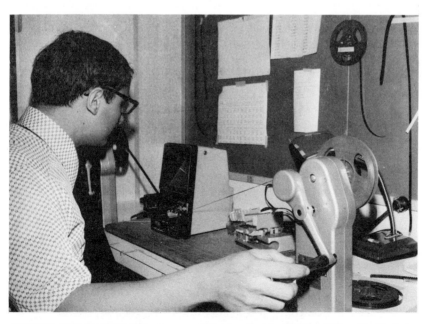

EDITING SUPER 8 FILM is a more delicate process than editing 16mm, but news staffers at KDUB-TV, Dubuque, have adapted to the narrower film.

exposure control, which means a separate meter reading is needed only in rare cases when you wish to override automatic control. The cameras are battery-operated, so there is no more winding. The battery also powers the zooming of the lens. When a filter is needed, you flip a switch instead of pulling one filter holder from a slot and replacing it with another as is done with many commonly used 16mm cameras. As Dick Neville, WGN-TV, Chicago, has put it, "The cameraman is suddenly free to become a reporter instead of a mechanic."

The cameras are so small and light that staffers at KDUB-TV, Dubuque, Iowa, routinely carry one with them, ready instantly to cover spot news. And it pays off. KDUB-TV Operations Manager Charles Cyberski was crossing a bridge one morning during a flash flood when he noticed a mobile home starting to cut loose. Up and into instant action went his camera, with exposure adjusting automatically. He caught the full movement of the mobile home breaking loose, charging downstream, and smashing into the bridge. Cyberski's film story was used on the ABC network that night.

Shooting sound film with super 8 is at least as easy as shooting with 16mm cameras. The Wilcam single-system sound camera used by KDUB-TV weighs less than 10 pounds loaded with 10 minutes of magnetic sound film and equipped with a 10:1 zoom lens. Don Sutherland wrote in *Popular Photography* (August, 1973, Vol. 73, No. 2, pp. 115, 140) of accompanying KDUB-TV Assignment Editor Dave Miller and Reporter Peter Roets on news assignments:

> I'd expected the news car to be glutted with a rearful of massive cases, tripods, and the sundry cables and accessories obliged for the proper exposure of film and optimum recording of sound. Instead, the newsmen slipped three small cases and a medium-weight tripod on the back seat. Off we went.
>
> Miller and Roets had just learned that a bank officer, also a member of the city council, was withdrawing his name from a list of political appointees, all to be accompanied by a touch of venom directed against certain political activities and individuals. Good newsmen maintain a demeanor of calm objectivity even in the face of a scoop, so as Miller and Roets entered the bank, nobody would have guessed there might be a buzz of excitement dashing about their heads. Nobody would have guessed even that they were a film crew if it weren't for the tripod, for their three compact cases could easily have contained valuables for sequester in a safe-deposit box.
>
> With complete production facilities in their hands, they entered a crowded elevator for the ride up to their subject's office. Roets went over some of the interview material with the officer while Miller set up the shot. Three ColorTran lights were quickly set, the Wilcam sound-on-film camera was loaded and mounted on the tripod. The 7-70mm zoom lens permitted a rather arbitrary camera-to-subject distance without compositional sacrifice, much to the newsmen's advantage in the already-cramped office.

The comparative silence of super 8 mechanism, coupled with a highly directional microphone, permitted a clean sound track even in these close quarters despite the lack of a soundproof camera blimp. Exposure readings were unnecessary because of the camera's behind-the-lens electric eye. Miller was ready to shoot before Roets had had the chance to straighten his tie.

The interview ran a few minutes, then was complete. Everybody shook hands, the newsmen struck their setup and packed everything away in their cases. Fifteen minutes after entering the bank, we were back in the news car with a significant story, in lip-synch and color, in the can. The remainder of the afternoon went similarly: casual, inconspicuous entrances, quick setups with the equipment easily accommodating difficult locations, successful takes . . . and swift departure.

Processing is the same for super 8 as for 16mm film, except that it does not take as long, because there is less footage to run through for the same amount of shooting time.

Editing is a little slower, at least at the start for the person used to handling 16mm. The narrower super 8 requires a finer touch in winding it through the viewer and splicing it. But persons who have edited quite a lot of super 8 say this is no great problem.

Super 8 transmission, of course, requires a special film projection chain. The signal also needs to run through an image enhancer, a device which heightens the resolution of the picture.

Easier Budgets

Dollars go much farther with super 8.

Equipment costs less than that for 16mm film or portable videotape. This means it is easier to provide each member of the staff with an individual camera to have on hand for spot news coverage. With super 8, it is also easier to find people in outlying areas who own equipment necessary for shooting film on an occasional free-lance or "stringing" basis.

The biggest savings come in film costs. The cost per minute of Eastman 7242 color film in 1974 was well under half as much for super 8 as for 16mm. The cost dropped to less than a third of 16mm for users of double super 8, a format in which a 100-foot spool which looks about like double-perforated 16mm film is flipped over after one pass through the camera and then split down the middle in processing to yield two spools of super 8.

Processing costs less. With less emulsion going through the tanks, less replenishing of solutions is required.

But What of Quality?

With so many advantages, why is super 8 not being used by more stations?

The smaller size carries its price. Because the image must be enlarged more, the super 8 picture tends to be softer both in focus and in color definition. Engineers have usually rated its quality as inferior to that of 16mm, though image enhancers have helped the quality.

The Future

If it can be demonstrated that super 8 yields consistent on-air quality comparable to that of 16mm, many newsrooms can be expected to move to the narrower film. RTNDA surveys have shown that budgets are news directors' biggest problems. If super 8 proves acceptable to station engineers and viewers, it should catch on in TV news.

Even without quality quite up to 16mm, super 8 can be expected to attract cable TV systems which originate local news. Economy is especially important for cable systems. Furthermore, some gain in quality may result from eliminating over-air transmission.

As this was being written, manufacturers were announcing new developments both in super 8 and portable electronic cameras. KDUB-TV, Dubuque, was continuing its research in both areas and had launched publication of a TV-oriented *Video/Film* magazine. News directors were taking a wait-and-see attitude, not wanting to invest in a new system only to have it rendered obsolete in a year or two.

New and better tools for reality reporting may number the days of the 16mm film which became the standard for television news from the start. Tomorrow's television camera reporter may carry all needed gear in a briefcase, and still have room for a bag lunch.

SUMMARY

Portable electronic cameras:
- Can provide live coverage of news.
- Can record events on videotape for faster playback than is possible with film.
- Records on videotape which can be reused to save on operating expenses.
- But, without expensive special equipment, videotape editing is slower than film editing.

Super 8 film:
- Is shot with highly portable equipment.
- Is less expensive than 16mm film.
- But picture quality has generally been inferior to 16mm.

11 | Trends: From Newsreel to News Reality

The Kentuckiana Newsreel was a big attraction on WHAS-TV, Louisville, in 1954. Channel 11's answer to the movie house newsreels of Movietone and Pathé came on much like the ones over at the Brown Theatre. Each newsreel story had a title, set on a title board, and there was music back of the silent film. It was always silent, as WHAS-TV did not own a sound-on-film camera then. The titles reflected film coverage prevalent in those days:

MAYOR SIGNS	VIADUCT	GROUND	PANCHO
ORDINANCE	FLOODED	BROKEN	FLIES IN

For 5–7 minutes, such film stories were run back to back, with the titles between. The Kentuckiana Newsreel followed and was not to be confused with "the news," which was a separate 5-minute package presented on-camera with perhaps some still pictures.

Television news changed greatly in the two decades that followed. By 1974, WHAS-TV and the profession generally had moved from newsreel to news reality. Newsfilm had long ago ceased to be just an added attraction, a "newsreel trailer." It had become television's primary tool for reporting the news. And most of the newsfilm of the 1970s on WHAS-TV and many other stations included sound as well as pictures of the news.

What will the future bring? We asked the persons in charge of newsfilm operations at stations with news directors who were members of RTNDA. (The methodology of the national survey conducted in 1973 for this book is described in the preface.) The responses, summarized in the table, indicate directions which leading professionals expected television newsfilm to take in the years ahead.

RESPONSES TO: "How much does your station use each of the following at present? And is the trend at *your* station toward using more, less or about the same of each?"

	Present use			Trend is toward		
	Much	Little	None	More	Less	Same
Natural SOF instead of silent	61%	38	1	87%	1	12
Voice ("talking head") SOF	66%	33	1	7%	65	28
Double projection ("B" roll)	68%	21	11	71%	1	28
Double system sound	9%	21	70	20%	7	73
Silent film of meetings	32%	65	3	4%	55	41
Film of spot events	86%	14	0	53%	4	43
Film of scheduled events	87%	13	0	17%	33	50
Film for in-depth reports	54%	45	1	71%	1	28
"Mini" docs within news	41%	55	4	72%	2	26
Documentary programs	33%	60	7	52%	6	43
On-scene reporter's voice-over	78%	20	2	53%	5	42
Available light indoors	28%	68	4	42%	10	48

Data from newsfilm survey conducted by Vernon Stone in summer 1973. Responses were received from 165 (71%) of 231 stations with news directors who were members of RTNDA.

More Natural SOF

The most impressive trend was toward the increased use of natural sound-on-film instead of silent film to communicate the reality of events and situations. Three-fifths of the stations said they were making "much" use of natural SOF, most others were shooting "some" of it, and an overwhelming 87% said they planned to replace more and more silent film coverage with natural SOF in the future. The shooting of natural sound has clearly become a necessary technique for the newsfilm camera-reporter.

Stations will have little choice but to include sound with pictures if they want to hold or compete for viewers. It did not take long in the transition from black-and-white to color for viewers to start feeling that something was missing when a story came on in black-and-white.

PANCHO FLIES IN, and beginning camera reporter Vernon Stone is at Standiford Field to cover the 1954 event for the Kentuckiana Newsreel for WHAS-TV, Louisville. Airport arrivals of celebrities such as the Cisco Kid's sidekick (Leo Carrillo) were big on the Kentuckiana Newsreel. The silent camera was the most used tool for TV newsfilm reporting in those days.

TWO DECADES LATER, television news was placing more effort on community problems than on celebrity arrivals, and portable sound cameras were becoming the primary tool for newsfilm reporting. Herb Gates films an interview by Connie Lockwood for WHIO-TV, Dayton.

Similarly, the more we see and hear natural SOF, the more we realize that something is missing when, for example, shots of a crowd or an assembly line come on in silence. Something IS missing—the sound which is part of the reality which television can communicate like no other news medium. Natural sound is becoming an essential part of that communication.

Less Time on Talking Heads

At the same time, we should continue to see less "voice" sound film. This is the so-called "talking head" film—for example, the city official sitting in an office telling a reporter about street problems. While two-thirds of the stations represented in the survey said they were showing lots of talking heads in 1973, two-thirds said they planned to cut back on this. And the trend was already well under way. Stations using relatively little voice SOF were the ones most likely to say they planned to use still less in the future.

More B-Roll

In place of talking heads, look for more use of B-roll, the second movie projector rolling off film showing those street problems (with natural SOF) while the city official talks about them on A-roll (the first projector) audio. Two-thirds of the stations surveyed said they were using "much" B-roll, and more than two-thirds said their trend was toward more use of B-roll. Interviews with city officials and others will continue to be shot. But more often, while listening to the interview on that film, we'll be seeing a second film (on the "B" projector) which shows the situation which is the topic of the interview.

With B-roll, as with some other progress areas treated in the survey, there was a tendency for the stations which were already the most progressive to say they planned to move ahead even further, while many of the others gave no indication that any change was planned. Three-fourths of the users of B-roll said they planned to use even more, but three-fourths of the non-users indicated that they had no plans to start using this double-projection newsfilm technique.

A Little More Double-System

Whereas double-projection (A and B rolls) refers to rolling two films at the same time with interspersed coordination of audio and video, double-system refers to a single film for which the picture is on a reel of film and the sound is on a separate reel of magnetic tape. Double-system permits more sophisticated editing than does the single-system (sound track on the same film with the picture) film most often used in television news. But the equipment necessary for efficient double-system editing is quite expensive.

The use of double-system was rather low at the time of the 1973 survey. Fewer than a third of the stations were using it at all. The 10% which were using "much" of it were happy with double-system and most planned to use more. Only a third of those using "little" planned to use more. Most stations which were using no double-system said they had no plans to start using it.

Less Silent Film of Meetings

That usually dull video—silent film coverage of meetings—appears on a continuing decline. Only a third of the operations surveyed reported using "much" of it, and more than half said they planned to use less. Silent film of visually routine meetings will not be missed in most cases.

But this silent footage may be with us in great quantities for a long time on a few stations. Whereas two-thirds of the low users said they planned to use even less, about half of the heavy users said they planned to use even more silent film of committees and other people sitting around tables. Thus a few stations in 1973 were just discovering the 1950s.

More Spot News Coverage

Viewers expect television coverage of important spot news events, and news directors realize it. When there is a flood, a major fire or a governmental crisis, people turn to television to see and hear the event. The survey showed most stations giving high priority to newsfilm coverage of spot events, and half saying their trend was toward even greater effort in this area. Most others planned to continue at existing levels.

Daybook Coverage Continuing

Scheduled events will continue to get heavy newsfilm coverage at the majority of stations. Most stations surveyed were making "much" use of such film in 1973. Half planned to continue at the present level, a sixth planned more, and a third said less. Several respondents planning reductions noted that they hoped to begin skipping more news conferences and speeches of marginal significance and such usually non-news "events" as ribbon-cuttings and groundbreakings.

More Depth Reports

Increased effort can be expected to go to depth reports, including the so-called "mini-documentaries" within regular newscasts. These are the special reports in which the station probes a situation and tells the story in film for 3 to 5 minutes or, at some stations, quite a bit longer. Most stations surveyed said they were doing at least some depth reports, and nearly three-fourths were looking forward to more of this.

More Documentaries?

Documentary programs as such have declined over the years. Our survey showed little activity in this area, but half of the respondents expected an upward trend. The main problem with documentary programs has been that they tend to compete poorly against entertainment programs on other channels. Many news directors argue that they get a better audience for depth reporting on an important topic by presenting it as an extended report or series of reports on regular news programs.

Letting Reporters Report

The trend in on-air reporting is to have film narrated by the reporter who covers the story, and quite often to show the reporter describing the event from the scene in a standup report. Whereas the Kentuckiana Newsreel of the 1950s was almost invariably narrated by the newscaster, the voice reports heard over newsfilm on WHAS-TV and many other stations in the 1970s were usually done by field reporters.

Three-fourths of the stations surveyed said they were making much use of "on-scene reporter's voice-over," and more than half expected to move more heavily in that direction. Many noted that they were working toward more newsfilm stories which are totally field-produced. The reporter describes the event from the scene, with natural SOF and B-roll utilized for true "actuality" film reporting.

More Use of Available Light

The trend toward greater realism in newsfilm includes increased use of available light for indoor filming. While fewer than a third of the stations surveyed were doing "much" indoor shooting without photo lights, two of every five said they planned to do more of this.

More Portable SOF Cameras

Prior to the 1970s, much television newsfilm work was severely limited by "portable" equipment which was not actually very portable. The Auricon sound cameras which most stations used remained much the same as the ones coming out of World War II, and most "portable" sound-on-film outfits were so heavy and awkward to hold that physical strength was as necessary as skill for one-person operation.

But lightweight, truly portable SOF cameras designed and built for the needs of television were available by 1973 and were the ones which the majority of survey respondents listed as their "preferred" cameras. The Cinema Products CP-16 and CP-16/A (described in Chapter 5) had been on the market for several months and were listed as the preferred cameras by more than half (57%) of the surveyed news operations. The Frezzi-Cordless LW-16 had just come on the market at the time of the survey, but by 1974 a number of leading stations were purchasing it. As this book went to press, these and other manufacturers were announcing still further breakthroughs in newsfilm technology.

The older Auricon conversions remained the most-used SOF cameras (by 61% of the stations) at the time of the survey, but were listed as the "preferred" cameras by only a fourth of the stations. The message was clear. To compete in the TV news market, a sound camera had to be designed for the needs of highly mobile field reporting—which means a lightweight, single-unit complete SOF outfit requiring only one person for operation.

Toward Live and Videotaped Coverage

The ultimate "tool" for television news reporting may be the electronic camera which can either transmit directly from the scene or feed into a back-strapped videotape recorder. Thanks in part to research and development performed for space shots, units like the Minicam have become available and are being refined constantly. A drawback has been the high cost of videotape editing facilities adequate for news needs, but computerized editing systems are being refined and can be expected to come down in price.

Only 3% of the stations in the 1973 survey were making much use of electronic cameras for news coverage, and 10% reported a "little" use. But at least half indicated they were considering the move to electronic cameras in place of film for field reporting as soon as technology and budgets permitted.

Super 8

Super 8, best known as home movie film, has been heralded for years as a potential replacement for the more expensive 16mm film which became the standard for television. The narrower film and its equipment are not only attractive in price but in reduced size and weight. However, because of its smaller image, super 8 film's technical quality has been inferior to 16mm film.

Not many stations expressed interest in super 8 in the RTNDA survey. Only two of 156 responding to that item said they were using super 8 film, 10% said they expected to use super 8 in the future, and 11% listed themselves as undecided. Advocates of super 8 foresaw continued improvement, but the extent to which it would catch on in television remained a question.

SPANNING THE YEARS since newsfilm began to appear on television in the 1940s, James Frezzolini, president of Frezzolini Electronics Inc., in the 1970s continued to spend more time in the lab than in the front office. He is shown working on the Frezzi-Cordless LW-16 sound camera. The father of the Frezzi-Lite was designing and producing newsfilm equipment in the early days of television.

Toward Understanding the Medium

Television news owes much of its impact to the audio-visual actuality—which usually means newsfilm—the pictures and sounds of events which make the viewer an eyewitness of the news. But too many practitioners remain insensitive to this medium as a true extension of the eyes and ears of people in living rooms. So an important step in learning to shoot, edit and write for these actuality films is to become aware of television's potential and limitations, then to use television as the medium it is rather than trying to imitate another medium of communication.

This is not newspaper. Try as you may, you will not be able to fill the front page of *The New York Times* with a transcript of your 22–25 minutes of news, weather and sports from a half-hour program. Don't try to be the *Times*. Your newscast will come off a poor imitation. Instead, place your emphasis on the audio-visual actuality which the *Times* can never hope to provide.

Television is not radio, though many in TV news treat it as little more than illustrated radio. These are the people who bring you such

THE FUTURE is expected to bring increased use of portable electronic cameras for TV news reporting. A WRC-TV (NBC), Washington, crew is shown getting ready for a late-breaking story. This one is to be recorded on videotape in the case on the back of the man on the left. But with relay by microwave or coaxial cable, the signal could be fed directly to the station for live coverage of the story. Newer equipment is becoming increasingly compact.

show-stoppers as the galloping voice report back of silent film of a city council meeting.

This is television, the medium of the full actuality, where viewers expect to witness the world around them and where no jobs are more important than the shooting, editing and producing of newsfilm reports.

So be yourself. You are not a newspaper writer or a radio writer-editor. You are a television journalist whose job is to shape smooth, tightly edited actuality reports from the raw material of film, tape and information.

The challenge is summarized by Jim Reiman, who served as a newsfilm photographer before becoming a reporter, then assignment editor, assistant news director, and finally news director at KOA-TV, Denver, and later news director at KRON-TV, San Francisco:

Television news is still faced with a majority of personnel who believe unwittingly that ours is a "radio" profession that incorporates film to make it more interesting. This is a syndrome developed years ago, and it still permeates our general approach to coverage of stories. The networks have offered most in cancelling that system, but become regularly trapped in presenting radio reports on television themselves.

The problem can be pinpointed to a minimum of film training for all but photographers and film editors. Few producers, reporters and writers have any real background in motion pictures as a medium for news.

A perfect television story would be one in which the film and natural sound tell the complete story without a word from a reporter. And it will never be accomplished without each person involved in the production of that story having complete and extensive knowledge of cinematography as applied to news.

Natural sound and natural film are what it is all about. The time required to go after, film and produce most news stories makes all of this difficult, but not always impossible.

Few professions exercise such ultimate professionalism at all times. Ours is no different, and words will always be a part of our business, especially in the context of their worth by "anchor-people." But the day will come when the "verbiage," as it is now used in all stories, will be as out of date as 1950s groundbreakings. When that kind of coverage becomes "habit," television news will have reached its ultimate.

SUMMARY

Key trends indicated by a survey conducted for this book:

- Natural SOF used more often in place of silent film.
- Less time showing "talking heads" and more using B-roll film to show situations they are talking about.
- Less silent film of meetings.
- Increases in already high levels of spot news coverage.
- More depth reports, more often as mini-documentaries and series in regular news programs than as separate documentary programs.
- More use of reporters' voices with the film of the stories they cover.
- More use of available light.
- Replacement of cumbersome old SOF cameras with ever-improving cameras which are truly portable.
- Increased use of live and videotaped reporting with portable electronic cameras.
- Replacement of the still too numerous newspaper and radio imitators with a new generation of television journalists who understand and can utilize the full potential of television as a medium for making the viewer an eyewitness to reality.

Appendix: RTNDA Code of Broadcast News Ethics

CODE OF BROADCAST NEWS ETHICS

RADIO TELEVISION NEWS DIRECTORS ASSOCIATION

The following Code of Broadcast News Ethics for RTNDA
was adopted January 2, 1966, and amended October 13, 1973.

*The members of the Radio Television News Directors Association agree
that their prime responsibility as journalists—and that of the broadcasting industry as the collective sponsor of news broadcasting—is
to provide to the public they serve a news service as accurate, full
and prompt as human integrity and devotion can devise. To that
end, they declare their acceptance of the standards of practice here set
forth, and their solemn intent to honor them to the limits of their
ability.*

ARTICLE ONE

The primary purpose of broadcast journalists—to inform the public of
events of importance and appropriate interest in a manner that is accurate and comprehensive—shall override all other purposes.

ARTICLE TWO

Broadcast news presentations shall be designed not only to offer timely and accurate information, but also to present it in the light of relevant circumstances that give it meaning and perspective.

> This standard means that news reports, when clarity demands it, will be laid against pertinent factual background; that factors such as race, creed, nationality or prior status will be reported only when they are relevant; that comment or subjective content will be properly identified; and that errors in fact will be promptly acknowledged and corrected.

ARTICLE THREE

Broadcast journalists shall seek to select material for newscast solely on their evaluation of its merits as news.

> This standard means that news will be selected on the criteria of significance, community and regional relevance, appropriate human interest, and service to defined audiences. It excludes sensationalism or misleading emphasis in any form; subservience to external or "interested" efforts to influence news selection and presentation, whether from within the broadcasting industry or from without. It requires that such terms as "bulletin" and "flash" be used only when the character of the news justifies them; that bombastic or misleading descriptions of newsroom facilities and personnel be rejected, along with undue use of sound and visual effects; and that promotional or publicity material be sharply scrutinized before use and identified by source or otherwise when broadcast.

ARTICLE FOUR

Broadcast journalists shall at all times display humane respect for the dignity, privacy and the well-being of persons with whom the news deals.

ARTICLE FIVE

Broadcast journalists shall govern their personal lives and such nonprofessional associations as may impinge on their professional activities in a manner that will protect them from conflict of interest, real or apparent.

ARTICLE SIX

Broadcast journalists shall seek actively to present all news the knowledge of which will serve the public interest, no matter what selfish, uninformed or corrupt efforts attempt to color it, withhold it or prevent its presentation. They shall make constant effort to open doors closed to the reporting of public proceedings with tools appropriate to broadcasting (including cameras and recorders), consistent with the public interest. They acknowledge the journalist's ethic of protection of confidential information and sources, and urge unswerving observation of it except in instances in which it would clearly and unmistakably defy the public interest.

ARTICLE SEVEN

Broadcast journalists recognize the responsibility borne by broadcasting for informed analysis, comment and editorial opinion on public events and issues. They accept the obligation of broadcasters for the presentation of such matters by individuals whose competence, experience and judgment qualify them for it.

ARTICLE EIGHT

In court, broadcast journalists shall conduct themselves with dignity, whether the court is in or out of session. They shall keep broadcast equipment as unobtrusive and silent as possible. Where court facilities are inadequate, pool broadcasts should be arranged.

ARTICLE NINE

In reporting matters that are or may be litigated, the journalist shall avoid practices which would tend to interfere with the right of an individual to a fair trial.

ARTICLE TEN

Broadcast journalists shall not misrepresent the source of any broadcast news material.

ARTICLE ELEVEN

Broadcast journalists shall actively censure and seek to prevent violations of these standards, and shall actively encourage their observance by all journalists, whether of the Radio Television News Directors Association or not.

Glossary

A-ROLL (used with B-roll). One of two reels of film running on projectors simultaneously, enabling the director to select audio or video from either reel. Normally the A-roll carries the primary audio and video and the B-roll carries video to go with part of the A-roll audio.

ACADEMY LEADER. Film leader showing a numerical countdown by seconds (8, 7, 6, 5, etc.), used to time cues for rolling film.

AMPLIFIER. An electronic device which boosts a sound signal (as from a microphone) to a level adequate for listening or recording.

APERTURE. Size of lens opening which admits light to film; also, sometimes used to refer to the iris diaphram, the lens part which changes size to regulate light entry.

ASA rating. An exposure index indicating the light sensitivity of a film.

AUDIO. The sound portion of a film or videotape; any sound.

AVAILABLE LIGHT. Indoors, the light from lamps, windows and other sources excluding TV lights.

B-ROLL. See "A-roll."

BACKGROUND. In video, the surroundings present in a scene; in audio, the incidental noise level.

BACK LIGHT. Supplemental light which shines on a subject from behind (and generally above). Helps subject visually stand out from background.

BALANCE STRIPE. A very narrow magnetic stripe adjacent to sprocket holes on magnetic film to help spool the film evenly on the reel.

BASE. The body of film, which holds emulsion and magnetic coatings; also refers to the side of film opposite the emulsion.

BLANK SCREEN. Absence of picture; can result from film running out early or from cutting a closing SOF segment on sound without providing picture to cover the final 1 second of sound.

BUSY. Crammed with detail.

BLOOP. To erase or cover unwanted sound on a film, audio tape or video-tape.

BOOM. A device, usually movable, to suspend a microphone near or above an audio source.

BRIDGE. In newsfilm, silent or natural sound film used between two segments of voice SOF; also, standup film of reporter between segments of film of the event or situation.

CHROMAKEY. An electric process by which a film, videotape or still picture can be made to appear behind a newscaster on the screen. The electronic image appears in place of a solid color backdrop.

CLOSEUP (CU). A shot filmed close to a subject to show detail.

COLOR TEMPERATURE. Color quality of a light source expressed in degrees Kelvin (K), essentially indicating the extent to which light is cool (bluish) like daylight or warm (reddish) like tungsten.

CONTINUITY. The smooth, logical flow of scenes or sounds to create the impression of a complete, unbroken action.

COPY. Written material (usually typed) which is read on the air.

CROPPING. The loss of picture area (oversweep) around the edges of film in television projection and transmission.

COVER. Film used to provide picture for the final 1 second of sound at the end of an SOF segment which has been cut on sound (which comes 28 frames before corresponding picture); also, film added at the end to give a director leeway in taking a segment's video off the screen.

CUE. A verbal or visual signal directing an action to be taken; also a physical signal on videotape or film which initiates an action, such as starting or stopping, automatically.

CUT. To edit film; also, a scene or portion of a longer film; also, the point where one shot joins another; also, a segment of film, e.g. SOF cut.

CUTAWAY. A scene, related to but not a part of the main action of a film sequence, which is placed between two scenes of the main action.

CUT-IN. A scene, related to and a part of the main action of a film sequence, usually a closeup of a detail contained in the immediately preceding scene of the main action.

CUT SHEET. In film editing-scripting, a sheet of paper on which exact times, descriptions and out-cues of film shots and sequences are noted.

DAYBOOK. A book in which scheduled news events for a day are listed. Folders, pads and chalk boards are also used.

DEAD SYNC. Positioning of a sound track immediately alongside the corresponding picture; done on magnetic striped film by use of a displacement recorder.

DEPTH OF FIELD. The range of distances in which a subject is in focus, e.g., objects 7-19 feet from the camera may be in focus when a 1-inch lens is set for 10 feet and f/4.

DISH. A round, normally concave antenna used to send or receive television signals by microwave between station and transmitter or between remote location and station.

DISPLACEMENT RECORDER. Equipment which can dub off and re-record film sound tracks to permit sound to be placed alongside picture in editing.

DISSOLVE. To fade out one scene, either electronically or by laboratory process in film, while fading in another.

DOLLY. To physically move a camera toward or from a subject.

DOUBLE-CHAIN. Two projectors running simultaneously to provide sound and picture as needed from two reels (A-roll and B-roll) of film.

DOUBLE-PERFORATED. Having sprocket holes along both film edges.

DOUBLE-PROJECTION. See "double-chain."

DOUBLE-SYSTEM. Sound recording in which a magnetic tape recorder running in synchronization with a camera records the audio portion while the film records the video portion; opposed to single-system, in which the sound is physically recorded on the same film as the picture.

DUB. To transfer video and/or audio from one film or tape to another.

EMULSION. The light-sensitive substance which coats one side of film and records the image.

ESTABLISHER. Opening of a film story which "sets the stage" for the story, establishing location, time or principal subjects.

EXPOSURE INDEX. A number indicating the light sensitivity of a film emulsion, usually expressed as an ASA rating, that can be used with exposure meters to help determine the correct exposure.

EXPOSURE METER. An instrument containing a photoelectric cell to measure the amount of light available for filming.

F/STOPS. On a lens, numerical indicators of aperture (size of opening letting in light).

FCC. The Federal Communications Commission, the agency which licenses and regulates radio and television broadcasting.

FPS. Frames per second at which film runs through a camera.

FADE. To diminish the intensity of an image electronically or photographically.

FAST. Film that is highly sensitive to light; also, a lens which opens to a very low f/stop.

FILL LIGHT. Supplemental light used to fill in shadows and reduce contrast from the key light.

FILM BIN. A receptacle into which ends of film are allowed to hang during the editing process.

FILM CHAIN. A complex of TV transmission equipment, generally containing one or more film projectors aimed into a TV camera so as to convert film images into electronic signals for broadcasting.

FILM TIMER (counter). An instrument which measures the length of film which is rolled through a sprocketed wheel called a gang.

FILM PLANE. The point in a camera (usually marked ϕ on the body) where film is positioned at the time of exposure.

FILTER. A piece of gelatin or glass placed in front of film to reduce the amount of light or modify the tone or color balance of light falling on the film.

FIRST DEVELOPER. In film processing, the chemical solution tank in which the basic developing takes place. It is here that any adjustments to compensate for incorrect exposure must be made.

FLASH FRAME. An overexposed frame or two sometimes found at the beginning or end of a shot, usually caused by the shutter remaining open between shots or the camera not reaching correct speed for a frame or two.

FORCE DEVELOPING. See "pushing."

FORMAT. The physical form—size, shape and medium—of presentation.

FRAME. A single still picture from motion picture film; also, the borders of a picture; also, to position a subject in relation to the borders of a picture.

FREEZE FRAME. The use of a single motion picture film frame as a still visual, created by stopping the projector or by laboratory printing and reprinting of the same frame.

FREZZI. Brand name for numerous items of Frezzolini motion picture equipment; sometimes used incorrectly as generic term for portable batteries and lights.

FULLCOAT. Film base with the full surface coated with a metallic oxide for magnetic recording of double-system sound.

GANG. A sprocketed wheel which film runs across in a timer or synchronizer.

GAIN. The loudness to which sound is amplified.

HANDOUT. In broadcast news, a film or tape provided to a station free by an outside source (government, industry, political candidate, etc.).

HOLD BACK. In processing, to reduce the time the film stays in the first developer; in effect, underdeveloping to compensate for overexposure.

IN AND OUT OF FRAME. A shooting technique in which the subject moves into and out of scenes while the camera remains stationary.

INCIDENT LIGHT READING. A measure of the amount of light falling upon (rather than reflected off) the subject to be filmed.

INTERCUT. In shooting or editing, to cut back and forth between film scenes of two or more separate but usually related actions.

JUMP CUT. A cut from one shot to the next in which a subject changes position abruptly for no apparent reason; usually from consecutive shots of roughly the same subject in the same activity filmed from the same position with the same lens.

KEY LIGHT. The principal light source, which establishes the exposure setting.

LAVALIER MIKE. A small microphone suspended around the neck or attached to clothing such as a tie.

LEADER. Blank or numbered film stock used to permit threading of a projector, to permit roll-through in the middle of a story, or to separate individual stories or segments on a single reel; also, film used at the beginning and end of a roll in loading and unloading a camera.

LEAD-IN. Copy introducing SOF or VTR with sound; also, newscaster's introduction to a newsfilm report.

LIBRARY FILM. Old film in the station's file.

LINE. Also called the 180° line, the real or imaginary division of a scene into two parts, which establishes screen direction.

LIP FLAP. Lip movement on the SOF image without accompanying sound, caused by the 28-frame gap between picture and matching sound; may occur at the beginning of a segment of single-system sound film.

LIP SYNC. Coordination of picture of lip movement with appropriate audio.

LIVE. Broadcast in real time, as it is happening.

LOOSE SHOT. Framing which leaves abundant space around the subject.

MAGAZINE. A light-tight container for film, either integral to the camera or capable of being attached; also, such a container into which film is loaded for processing.

MAGNETIC SOUND. Sound recorded on magnetic (metallic oxide) stripe which runs along the base side of motion picture film.

MATCH-CUT. Two adjoining shots containing an action which appears to be continuous, best filmed from different distances or angles.

MATCH-REVERSE. Following an action in one direction until it meets an action going the opposite direction and then following the second action back the other way.

MEDIUM SHOT (MS). Framing which shows a moderate amount of the subject, in contrast to a closeup (CU) or long (LS) view.

MICROWAVE. An electromagnetic wave by which television signals may be relayed through the air from a transmitter to a receiving station.

MIX. To blend sound or picture from two or more sources.

MONOPOD. A single pole attached to the base of a camera for steadying.

MONTAGE. A rapid succession of non-sequential shots, usually very short, used to create a mood or impression; need not have visual continuity.

NATURAL SOUND. Actual sound of an event, situation or process (riot, traffic, assembly line, etc.) recorded directly on sound film. Does not refer to sound primarily of people talking (voice sound).

NEUTRAL DENSITY. A filter to reduce the intensity of light reaching film without affecting the tonal rendition of colors in scenes.

NEWS DIRECTOR. The person in charge of a radio or television news operation.

NORMAL LENS. A lens which puts an image on a particular film format in roughly the same perspective as viewed by the human eye; a lens with focal length equal to the diagonal measure of the film format used, e.g. a 25mm (1-inch) lens for 16mm film.

OPTICAL SOUND. Seldom used in TV news, sound recorded via light images on a track along the edge of the film (rather than on magnetic stripe).

OVERSHOOT. A glaring effect in transmission caused by a film chain's automatic shader reacting to a sudden change of light intensity, usually a result of putting a very dark scene next to a very light scene.

OVERSWEEP. Picture lost (about 10% around the edges) in TV projection and transmission. Also "cropping."

OVER-THE-SHOULDER. Shooting past the rear of one person's head (usually a reporter) to a scene or another person.

OUT CUE. The words with which a film or VTR segment ends.

OUTTAKES. Film shot but not used in the finally edited story.

PACE. To shoot or edit scene length to fit the mood of a story.

PAD SHOT. Extra film at the end of a story to provide adequate video for an overly long script or to permit a slow fade-out or dissolve.

PAN. To turn a camera from one position to another while shooting.

PARALLAX. The lateral difference between the field of view of a non-reflex viewfinder and that of the shooting lens; critical at short distances.

POOP SHEET. A written account of shots, identifications and other information which might be needed in editing and scripting a film story.

PORTABLE LIGHTS. Usually refers to battery-operated lights which can be attached to a camera.

PRESENCE. Background noise present in a location and audible on a sound track.

PROCESSOR. The machine in which film is developed.

PUSHING. To compensate for underexposure by overdeveloping film during processing.

RTNDA. Radio Television News Directors Association, an international professional organization of broadcast journalists.

REACTION SHOT. A scene which demonstrates a reaction to an action shown in the preceding scene; many cutaways are reactions shots.

REFLECTED LIGHT READING. A measure of the amount of light bouncing off the subject.

REFLEX VIEWING. Viewing the scene directly through the lens of a camera rather than through a separate optical device.

REVERSAL. Typically in sound-on-film work, a shot of the interviewer from the interviewee's point of view.

REVERSAL FILM. Film that comes out of the processor with a positive image; most TV newsfilm is reversal rather than negative.

REWINDS. Upright devices placed on both sides of a viewer to hold film for winding and rewinding during editing.

ROLL-THROUGH. A portion of film or videotape which runs unseen and unheard to avoid stopping a projector or tape machine.

ROUGH CUT. First-stage editing of film scenes into approximate order and length of use; ends are usually taped together rather than spliced at this stage, which is often omitted in busy newsrooms.

SOF. Sound-on-film.

SCREEN DIRECTION. The direction of real or implied motion in a film story, related to the way the viewer sees it, i.e., left-to-right, right-to-left or neutral (movement directly into or away from camera).

SEQUENCE. An arrangement of shots in a logical order to show progression or development of action in apparent chronological order.

SETUP LIGHTS. TV lights normally mounted on stands and plugged into AC electrical outlets.

SHADER. In TV projection and transmission, a device, often set for automatic operation, to balance light intensity of the TV picture (video) to a moderate level within and across scenes.

SHOT. Generally, a continuous piece of film from the starting of the camera to the stopping of the camera.

SHOTGUN MICROPHONE. A long, highly directional microphone used for isolating sounds at a distance.

SHOULDER POD. A device which may be attached to a camera to rest it on a shoulder. The part touching the shoulder is usually curved and padded.

SINGLE-PERFORATED. Having sprocket holes along only one of the two film edges.

SINGLE-SYSTEM. SOF shooting in which the sound is physically recorded on the same film as the picture.

SLOW. Film which requires relatively intense light for exposure; also, a lens which does not open to a very low f/stop.

SOFT. Not in sharp focus.

SOUND BITE. A segment of sound-on-film.

SOUND-ON-FILM. Film with a sound track.

SOUND READER. A small device through which sound-on-film is run in editing. A pickup head wired to an amplifier-speaker permits the editor to listen to the film's sound track.

SOUND TRACK. The path or stripe on film or tape on which sound is recorded.

SPEED. The rate at which film runs through a camera, measured in frames per second (fps); also, the light sensitivity of film, usually expressed as an ASA rating.

SPLICE. The physical connection of two pieces of film or tape.

SPLICER. A device for joining two pieces of film or tape.

STANDUPPER. An on-the-scene report in which a reporter is filmed while telling the story to the camera.

STOCK. Raw (unexposed, unprocessed) film.

STOP DOWN. To reduce the amount of light reaching the film by reducing the size of the lens aperture, thus going to a higher f/stop.

SUPER. The electronic superimposition of one image upon another, generally used in newsfilm production for visual word identification of locations, speakers, etc., usually at the bottom of the screen.

SUPER 8. Film which is 8 millimeters wide but which uses smaller perforations and a larger image area than regular 8mm film.

SYNC SIGNAL (sync pulse). In double-system filming, an electrical impulse recorded on a magnetic tape sound track to indicate points of synchronization between separate tracks, as for the picture on film and the sound on a separate audio tape.

SYNCHRONIZER. In editing, a timer with two or more gangs permitting two or more films, either picture or sound track, to be drawn through in synchronization with each other.

TAKE. A shot; also, the point in a story or program at which film or other material is "taken" for on-air use.

TAKE LENS. The lens on a turret which is in the shooting position.

TALKING HEAD. Usually a head and shoulders shot of a newsmaker talking about a situation; often visually dull.

TELEPHOTO LENS. A lens with a narrow angle of view and long focal length (greater than 25 mm for 16mm cameras).

TIGHT SHOT. Framing with little or no space around a subject.

TILT. A vertical pan.

TIME-BASE CORRECTOR. An electronic device for correcting instability in an image recorded on videotape.

TRACK. See "sound track."

TRIPOD. A three-legged stand which holds a camera.

TRUCK. To physically move a camera parallel to the direction of movement of a subject.

TURRET. A part of a camera body on which lenses (usually 3) can be mounted, with the turret rotated to put a desired lens into shooting position.

UPCUT. To accidentally overlap two sources of sound, e.g. narration running over onto the start of a sound segment.

VTR. Videotape recording.

VIDEO. The visual portion of a film or videotape story; anything "seen" on television.

VIDEOTAPE. Magnetic tape which records both sound and picture.

VIEWER. In editing, a device through which film is wound for projection of the image on a small glass screen.

VIEWFINDER. An optical element of a camera through which the photographer views scenes.

VOICE OVER (VO). A voice description by a reporter or newscaster while film or other visual material is on the screen.

WIDE ANGLE. A lens giving a wide view of scenes, with focal length less than 25mm for 16mm cameras.

WILD SOUND. Sound recorded on audio tape not synchronized with the camera.

WINDSCREEN. A cover placed over a microphone to reduce wind noise.

WIPE. An electronic process in which one scene appears to "wipe" another scene from the screen.

WRAPAROUND. Narration leading into or out of SOF.

ZOOM. A lens with variable focal length; also, to change focal length of such a lens during a shot.

Index